The Christian Girl's Guide to
The Bible

LEGACY PRESS®

www.LegacyExpress.com

Check out all of the books in
The Christian Girl's Guide series:

The Christian Girl's Guide to Being Your Best

The Christian Girl's Guide to Friendship

The Christian Girl's Guide to the Bible

The Christian Girl's Guide to Your Mom

The Christian Girl's Guide to Money

The Christian Girl's Guide to Change

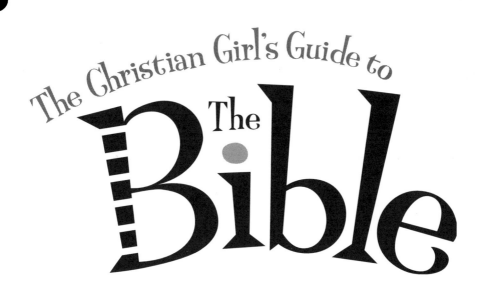

The Christian Girl's Guide to The Bible

Katrina Cassel

Dedication

To Rick for always believing in me.

To Tyler and Jessica who read the pages, tried the puzzles and gave me lots of kid-input on the book.

To Teresa for all her suggestions.

To Dr. Ronald Manahan for making the Old Testament come alive for his students.

THE CHRISTIAN GIRL'S GUIDE TO THE BIBLE
©2010 by Katrina Cassel, twelfth printing
ISBN 10: 1-58411-044-9
ISBN 13: 978-1-58411-044-6
Legacy reorder# LP48213
JUVENILE NONFICTION / Religion / Christianity / Christian Life

Legacy Press
P.O. Box 261129
San Diego, CA 92196
www.LegacyExpress.com

Mixed Sources
Product group from well-managed forests and other controlled sources
www.fsc.org   Cert no. GFA-COC-001990
©1996 Forest Stewardship Council
FSC

Interior Illustrator: Aline Heiser
Cover Illustrator: Anita DuFalla

Scriptures are from the *Holy Bible: New International Version* (North American Edition), ©1973, 1978, 1984 by the International Bible Society. Used by permission of Zondervan Bible Publishers.

Printed in the United States of America

Table of Contents

Chapter 1 : The Bible Is for You............................7

Chapter 2 : Moses' Messages 25

Chapter 3 : Heroes in History.............................58

Chapter 4 : Songs and Sayings 89

Chapter 5 : Prophetic Announcements Part 1......100

Chapter 6 : Prophetic Announcements Part 2......112

Chapter 7 : Gospel Gems 124

Chapter 8 : Apostles in Action 151

Chapter 9 : Learning from the Letters 163

Chapter 10 : Exciting Endtimes 186

Puzzle Answers 191

Introduction

Hi! Welcome to The Christian Girl's Guide to the Bible! The Bible is an awesome book. But it's more than just a book: it's God's Word!

In the Bible you'll find heroes and villains, action stories, love stories and lessons for living your faith every day. You'll learn about the first people God created, about kings and prophets and about fishermen and preachers. You'll find out how the church began. But the most important thing about the Bible is that it teaches you about Jesus.

The Christian Girl's Guide to the Bible will help you understand when and how the Bible was written. Then it will take you through the Bible a section at a time from Genesis to Revelation. You'll learn important truths from the Bible. You'll also be able to take quizzes, solve puzzles and codes, and do crafts and activities.

I hope you will learn a lot from this book and have fun doing it!

Katrina Cassel
Callaway, Florida

Chapter One

The Bible Is for You!

Katelynn opened the box her grandmother gave her. It was a Bible with her name engraved in gold on the cover. She flipped through it and saw many pictures of Bible stories she knew. In the back of the Bible, there were maps and charts. She had never had a book with 990 pages before!

"I thought it was time for you to have your own Bible," her grandmother said. "Do you know why the Bible is important?"

"Because it's God's Word?" Katelynn said.

"That's right," her grandmother answered. "The Bible is how we know what God wants us to do. It's like a road map for how we should live."

Does your family use an atlas when you travel? Perhaps your dad uses a map to plan a route ahead of time. Or maybe your mother stops along the road to check that she is still on the right highway. It's helpful to have something to look at to tell you how to get to your destination. The Bible is like that–it guides you in your faith.

In this book, you will learn about all of the books in the Bible, but first you'll learn some things about the Bible itself. You'll learn when and how it was written. You'll find out who wrote it and how they did it without making mistakes.

How much do you really know about the Bible? Take the quiz on the next page to find out.

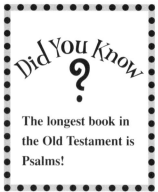

Did You Know?

The longest book in the Old Testament is Psalms!

The Bible Is for You!

 Answer It

Am I a Bible Brain?

Choose the correct answer to each question.
Don't be discouraged if you don't know
some of the answers because you will
by the end of this book!

1 How many books are in the Bible?
a. 22
b. 66
c. 33

2 How many books are in the Old Testament?
a. 18
b. 52
c. 39

3 How many books are in the New Testament?
a. 15
b. 27
c. 36

4 Who wrote the most books of the Bible?
a. John
b. Paul
c. Daniel

5 About how many different people wrote books of the Bible?
a. 40
b. 10
c. 100

6 The Old Testament was originally written in what language?
a. English
b. Greek
c. Hebrew

7 The New Testament was originally written in what language?
a. English
b. Greek
c. Hebrew

The word "testament" means what?
a. covenant or agreement
b. book
c. god

 The first books of the Bible were written in about what year?
a. 1400 BC
b. 100 BC
c. 95 AD

 About when did John write the book of Revelation?
a. 4,000 BC
b. 100 BC
c. 95 AD

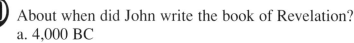 The word "inspired" means what?
a. God-breathed
b. written by man
c. born of God

 The word "infallible" means what?
a. old book
b. without error
c. written by God

13 The word "illumination" means what?
a. The work of the Holy Spirit that allows us to understand the Bible.
b. Guarded from all errors
c. Words are from God

14 The word "revelation" means what?
a. The Bible is a special book.
b. God shows himself to man through the Bible.
c. Men revealed themselves in their writings.

Check your answers !

1. b	7. b	13. a
2. c	8. a	14. b
3. b	9. a	
4. b	10. c	
5. a	11. a	
6. c	12. b	

How well did you do?

11-14 correct: You are a Bible genius!

7-10 correct: You are a Bible pro.

4-6 correct: You are a Bible beginner.

Less than 4 correct: Whew! Good thing you're reading this book!

The Old and New Testaments

Nicole stepped into her new classroom and looked for a desk with her name on it. She saw it in the front corner. Walking over to it, she put her books inside and then sat down. She looked around the room. Nicole loved the first day of school. Everything seemed bright and new.

Mrs. Knight walked to the front of the classroom. "Good morning," she said. "And welcome to sixth grade. I know we are going to have a great year. First, let's go over some classroom rules."

Mrs. Knight began writing rules on the chalkboard. When she finished, she read all 10 aloud to the class.

"These rules are firm," she said. "There will be no arguing about them. If you follow these rules, then I will be able to teach you all you need to learn this year. And if you follow the rules well, we will have a special activity each Friday afternoon. Do we have an agreement?"

"Yes," Nicole answered along with the other students.

Describe an agreement you have made with your parents or someone else.

_____

_____

Did both sides keep the agreement?

_____

God made covenants, or agreements, with his people throughout Bible times. Sometimes the people didn't keep their part of the agreements, but God always did.

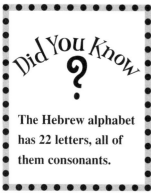

Did You Know?

The Hebrew alphabet has 22 letters, all of them consonants.

The Bible is broken into two major divisions called the Old Testament and the New Testament. The word "testament" means "covenant." In the Old Testament, God made a covenant to bless the Israelites as His special people. They were to worship only Him and to accept His laws. To be forgiven of sins, they had to sacrifice animals.

In the New Testament, Jesus was the covenant. In the Upper Room, Jesus told His followers, "This cup is the new covenant in my blood, which is poured out for you" (Luke 22:20). People no longer offered animals for sacrifices. Jesus became the sacrifice for sin.

The Bible has 66 books. The Old Testament is made up of 39 books and the New Testament contains 27 books. Many of the books of the New Testament were letters that Paul wrote to churches and certain people.

The Old Testament was written mostly in Hebrew with a few sections in Aramaic. The New Testament was written in Greek.

It's all Greek to me!

 Answer It

Books of the Bible

How well do you know the books of the Bible? The book in the middle of each pair below is missing. Try to fill in the name of the missing book without looking at the list in the front of your Bible.

1 Genesis _____ Leviticus

2 Numbers _____ Joshua

3 Judges _____ 1 Samuel

4 Ezra _____ Esther

5 Job _____ Proverbs

6 Ezekiel _____ Hosea

7 Haggai _____ Malachi

8 Matthew _____ Luke

9 John _____ Romans

10 Galatians _____ Philippians

11 Titus _____ Hebrews

12 3 John _____ Revelation

> **Did You Know?**
>
> Parts of the original Bible were written on papyrus, a reed-like plant. Strips of papyrus were soaked and woven together. When they dried they formed "paper."

Check your answers on the next page!

1. Exodus	7. Zechariah
2. Deuteronomy	8. Mark
3. Ruth	9. Acts
4. Nehemiah	10. Ephesians
5. Psalms	11. Philemon
6. Daniel	12. Jude

Did you get all 12 correct? Good for you! You are on your way to being a Bible scholar. If you missed some, practice saying the books of the Bible each day until you memorize them.

How to Look Up a Verse in the Bible

Bible references look like this: **John 3:16.**

The first thing in the reference is the **book** of the Bible. Once you learn the books of the Bible in order, it will be easy to find each book quickly. If you don't know the books of the Bible by memory, you can look at the list in the front of your Bible. Find the book of John and the page number, then flip to John.

The first number–3 in this case–is the **chapter number**. In your Bible, chapter numbers will be printed larger than verse numbers. Find the book of John, then look for the big number 3.

The second number is the **verse number**. A colon (:) separates chapter numbers from verse numbers. Find John chapter 3, then slide your finger down the smaller numbers until you find 16. The verse should start, "For God so loved the world."

Sometimes references can look very confusing. Here are examples:

John 3-4   Because there is no colon, this is John chapters 3 through 4.

John 3:16-21   Because there is a colon between the 3 and the 16 this means John chapter 3, verse 16 through verse 21.

John 3:16-4:10 The dash between 3:16 and 4:10 means that you should read all the way from chapter 3, verse 16, to chapter 4, verse 10.

Looking up verses may seem confusing, but it will get easier as you do it!

Meet the Bible Authors

The books of the Bible were written by over 40 men from kings to fisherman, doctors to tax collectors. The authors of some Bible books are not known. Some Bible scholars have tried to use clues from the books to guess their authors, but the scholars don't always agree. We will give the authors more attention later in this book, but for now try the quiz below.

👉 Do It

The men who wrote the Bible weren't originally writers. They had other jobs. Match each Bible author below with his job. You will use some answers more than once. If you don't know the job for a Bible character, just look up the Bible reference after his name.

___ 1. David (1 Samuel 16:11-13) ___ 6. Nehemiah (Nehemiah 2:1)

___ 2. Matthew (Matthew 9:9) ___ 7. Amos (Amos 1:1)

___ 3. Luke (Colossians 4:14) ___ 8. Habakkuk (Habakkuk 1:1)

___ 4. Peter (Matthew 4:18) ___ 9. Solomon (1 Kings 1:39)

___ 5. Paul (Acts 18:1-4) ___ 10. Moses (Exodus 3:1)

    a. doctor   b. prophet

    c. king   d. tent maker

    e. shepherd   f. fisherman

    g. tax collector   h. cupbearer to the king

Answers

1. c or e	2. g	3. a	4. f	5. d
6. h	7. e	8. b	9. c	10. e

Did you know most of these? If you did, great! If not, that's okay. You can always learn something new about the Bible.

An Old New Book

Megan pulled a book from her grandmother's bookshelf. The cover was worn and cracked. Megan opened the book and tried to read one of the yellowed pages.

"Grandma, this doesn't make sense," Megan said. "I don't understand what this is saying."

"That's because it's a very old book," her grandmother explained. "People don't speak like that any longer. I'm not even sure what some of the words mean! I've kept the book because it's been passed down through the generations in our family."

The Bible is also a very old book, but unlike the book Megan found, the Bible speaks to us just as much as it did to its first readers.

The first books of the Bible were written about 1400 years before Christ was born. The whole Old Testament was finished around 400 years before Christ's birth. How long did it take for the whole Old Testament to be written? (hint: subtract)

_____

All of the books of the New Testament were written between 40 AD and 95 AD. How long did it take for the whole New Testament to be written? (hint: subtract)

_____

The Old Testament covers a lot of history. The New Testament tells mostly about Jesus' life and ministry and the growth of the early church. The Old and New Testaments were carefully copied and kept safe. At first, each book was just one long book. Later, chapters and verses were added to make it easier to find the different stories and teachings.

Four Important Words

Reading and learning about the Bible isn't difficult, but there are four words that are hard to understand at first.

Inspiration

Rebecca sat in a circle at her friend Megan's birthday party. "We're going to play a game called 'telephone'," Megan's mother said. "I'm going to whisper something to Megan and she will whisper it to Erin and so on until we whisper it all the way around the circle. Then we'll see if what the last person heard is the same as what the first person heard."

Megan's mother whispered something in Megan's ear and the game began. Finally the last person heard the message. "I think she said, 'next week my bad Aunt Pam is coming for me'."

Megan hooted with laughter and so did Erin. "No, it was 'Once I had a black cat named Sam," she said.

"You said, 'Sam'?" Erin asked. "I thought you said Pam."

"And I thought Erin said 'aunt' not cat," Rebecca said.

"And by the time everyone heard it a little bit wrong, it became totally wrong," Megan's mom said.

Did You Know **?**

"BC" means the years Before Christ. Count backwards to find BC years. For example, 400 BC happened 400 years before Christ was born, and 100 BC happened 100 years before Christ was born, so 400 BC comes before 100 BC.

That was just a game at a party, but what if the men writing the Bible each got the stories or the teachings just a little wrong? That would make a big difference! That's why God inspired the Bible.

Inspiration means "God-breathed." 2 Timothy 3:16 in the NIV says, "All scripture is God-breathed." In the King James it says, "All scripture is given by inspiration of God." That's how the men knew what to write when they wrote parts of the Bible. Moses wrote about the creation of the world but he wasn't there when it happened. God must have told him about it so he could write it down. This doesn't mean that God told the authors the exact words to say. He let their personalities show in their writings.

Infallible

"Oh, I hate when they do that," Terra said, sticking a bookmark in her book and setting it down.

"What do you hate?" her mom asked.

"When the details don't match in a book! At the beginning of the book it said the girl broke her left arm playing soccer and then later it said she couldn't write a letter to her grandmother with her right arm in a cast! now, if she broke her left arm, then what is her right arm doing in a cast?" Terra demanded.

"I know what you mean," her mom agreed. "I just read a detective story where the detective dropped her keys on her car floor in the dark. Then a little later she is captured and tied up in her house. She uses her car keys to help her get loose. How can she use the car keys when they are outside in her car?"

Have you ever found a mistake in a book you read? What was it?

_____

_____

Books we read sometimes have parts that don't fit together. But God's book, the Bible, is **infallible**. That means the Bible doesn't have any mistakes. Because God told the authors what to write and because God is perfect, His Word is also perfect. If the authors wrote the Bible on their own, we would probably find many errors as Terra and her mother did.

Sometimes people think things in the Bible are wrong. That is either because of an error people made translating the Bible from Hebrew or Greek to English, or because we don't understand enough about Bible times and customs. The Bible is never wrong.

Illumination

Misty sat on her bed staring at a magazine. "I don't get it. I just see a picture of a forest. It says there is supposed to be a tiger in this picture, but I don't see it."

"Oh, I saw that in my magazine too," her friend Amy said. "Here, turn on your desk lamp. now hold the page like this."

Amy turned the magazine so the light shone across the picture.

"I see it now," Misty said. "That's cool. I can't believe I didn't see it before."

"That's because you didn't have the light shining on it," Amy said. "You can't see it without the light."

Illumination is the work of the Holy Spirit that allows us to understand the Bible. It's like when the light shone on Misty's magazine. Without the light, Misty didn't see the picture. When people try to read the Bible without God's help, it doesn't make sense to them. 1 Corinthians 2:14 says, "The man without the Spirit does not accept the things that come from the Spirit of God, for they are foolishness to him, and he cannot understand them, because they are spiritually discerned."

Jesus told his disciples "But the Counselor, the Holy Spirit, whom the Father will send in my name, will teach you all things and will remind you of everything I have said to you" (John 14:26). Jesus also said, "But when he, the Spirit of truth, comes, he will guide you into all truth" (John 16:13). The Holy Spirit is the one who helps us understand what we read in the Bible.

Revelation

"I have a prize for all of you who said today's verse," Mrs. Foster told her Sunday school class. "These are books of hidden pictures. The pages look blank, but when you color over one with a pencil, a picture appears."

Morgan thanked Mrs. Foster for her book and began coloring over the first page. "Cool. It's a picture of Jesus," Morgan said.

There are many ways to reveal–or show–things. Morgan revealed the picture of Jesus by coloring over a page. Psalm 19:1 tells us that the glory of the stars shows us God. The Bible also shows us God.

God chose to use His Word to reveal Himself to people. We learn more about God as we read further into the Bible. By studying the whole Bible, we get a clearer picture of who God is. But each time we read the Bible we will learn something new. We can never learn all there is to learn in the Bible.

Find the Right Bible for You

If you walk into a Christian bookstore, or into the book section of a discount store, you'll find many different kinds of Bibles.

The King James Bible (KJV) was published in 1611. Many people still use it today. But you might find the language hard to understand. Other versions of the Bible have come along since then. The verses in this book are from the New International Version (NIV) of the Bible published in 1978. Many Bible scholars used the best Hebrew, Aramaic and Greek texts still available to translate the Bible and to use words that we understand  better today. There is also a New King James version (NKJV) that has updated language in it.

There are versions that are even easier to read such as the International Children's Bible (ICB) or the New International Reader's Version (NIrV). Among the different versions of the Bible, there are specialty Bibles made just for kids your age. They each have different features designed to explain life in Bible times, answer questions, explain hard words and so on.

Still confused? Here is some advice from girls who found Bibles they like.

> I like the International Children's Bible because it's easy to read and it has a lot of good pictures of different Bible stories. My Bible is pink and has my name engraved on it.
>
> ~ Jessica, age 11

> I have a New International Version of the Bible. I like it better than the King James version because I can understand it better. I read it every day. My parents help me understand why God did this and why he did that.
>
> ~ Katey, age 9

My Bible is an Adventure Bible. I like how it's laid out and the pictures help me understand the Bible better.

~ Leah, age 8

I have an Explorers Bible. It's got good stuff in it like words you can actually understand. It includes little Bible hero riddles that are fun. It also has boxes that say what different Bible characters learned. The neat part is that it's written like they are talking to me.

~ Abby, age 10

My Bible is a New King James Version. When you read a story it says where it happened [location]. Then you can look in the back of the Bible at the map and find out exactly where it was.

~ Andrea, age 12

Why Read the Bible

Choosing a Bible is not as important as actually sitting down and reading it! Why is reading the Bible important? 2 Timothy 3:16-17 says, "All Scripture is God-breathed and is useful for teaching, rebuking, correcting and training in righteousness, so that the man of God may be thoroughly equipped for every good work."

The Bible teaches us about God and the Christian life. It teaches what we should believe about heaven, salvation, baptism and other important things.

Look up John 20:31 in your Bible. Why does it say we have the Scriptures?

The Bible points out our sins. It shows us what is right and wrong. The Bible talks about a holy God who hates sin. It also shows us the correct ways to act.

Look up Psalm 119:11. What is a good reason to learn God's Word?

_____

What does Psalm 119:105 say the Bible can do for us?

_____

The Bible trains us in righteousness and prepares us to do the things God wants us to do.

To what does Peter compare the Bible in 2 Peter 1:19?

_____

What does Hebrews 4:12 say the Bible judges?

_____

What does James 1:23-25 say a person is like who sees the problems in his life by reading the Bible but doesn't correct them?

_____

Wow! Do you see what an important book the Bible is? Over 40 men who didn't even all live at the same time wrote it. But God made sure that each man wrote the right message. The Bible was written over a thousand years ago, but it still tells us how to live today. And when we read it and live it, God blesses us!

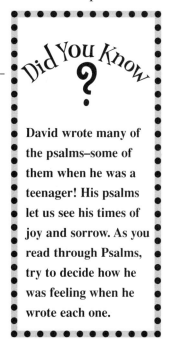

Did You Know?

David wrote many of the psalms–some of them when he was a teenager! His psalms let us see his times of joy and sorrow. As you read through Psalms, try to decide how he was feeling when he wrote each one.

 Make It

My Bible Bag

The Bible is such an important book that we need to treat it carefully. So why not make a bag in which to keep your Bible and other items such as a Bible journal or notebook? You can use it at home and you can take it to church.

The Bible shows us how to walk with God so the instructions below tell you how to write that on your bag, but you don't have to. You can write anything you want and decorate it in a way that feels right to you!

What You Need

* plain cloth bag (from craft store)
* puff paints
* craft paint
* shallow dish
* sponge
* scissors
* blow dryer

What to Do

1. Write "Walk With God" on the front of the bag with puff paints.
2. Allow the bag to dry overnight.
3. Draw a small foot on the sponge and cut it out so you have a foot-shaped sponge.
4. Pour a small amount of craft paint into a shallow dish.
5. Dip the footprint sponge into the paint.
6. Blot the sponge on a piece of paper, then press it onto your bag. Make as many footprints as you want. Add other designs or decorations if you want.
7. Blow hot air from a hair dryer on the dried paint until you see it puff up.
8. Enjoy using your special Bible bag!

Chapter Two

Moses' Messages

The Old Testament is like a whole library! It has history, laws, rules for living, genealogies (lists of grandparents, great grandparents and so on), stories, poetry and prophecies.

The 39 Old Testament books are divided into different categories.

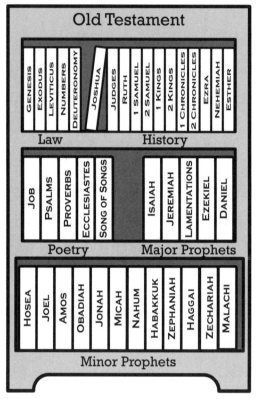

Law Books
Genesis
Exodus
Leviticus
Numbers
Deuteronomy

History Books
Joshua
Judges
Ruth
1&2 Samuel
1&2 Kings
1&2 Chronicles
Ezra
Nehemiah
Esther

Poetry Books
Job
Psalms
Proverbs
Ecclesiastes
Song of Songs

Major Prophet Stories
Isaiah
Jeremiah
Lamentations
Ezekiel
Daniel

Minor Prophet Stories
Hosea
Joel
Amos
Obadiah
Jonah
Micah
Nahum
Habakkuk
Zephaniah
Haggai
Zechariah
Malachi

Do It

Fill in the grid below with the Old Testament books listed. Some letters are filled in to help you.

Amos

Daniel

Deuteronomy

Esther

Exodus

Genesis

Habakkuk

Isaiah

Joshua

Judges

Leviticus

Nahum

Nehemiah

Psalms

Ruth

See the finished puzzle on page 191

The Law Books

Moses wrote the law books. The first one is Genesis. It starts with the creation of the world. Since Moses wasn't there to see God create the world, we know that God must have told him what to write.

Genesis

The word "Genesis" means "beginnings" and Genesis really is a book of beginnings. Genesis covers many important events and people: Creation, Noah and the Flood, the Tower of Babel, Abraham, Jacob and Esau and Joseph. Read on to find out more about what happens in Genesis.

Creation (Genesis 1:1–2:2)

Have you ever walked into a dark room and couldn't see anything at all? Maybe it seemed like the room was empty and you were totally alone. That might be what it was like before God started His wonderful work of creation. The Bible tells us that when God created the earth it was empty and dark. That wouldn't have been a nice place to live! But God didn't leave it that way. He created many wonderful things. Do you remember what God made on each day of creation? Put the correct letter before each number to match what was created to the day it was created.

☞ Do It

Order the Days

___ 1. Day one	a. Sun, moon, and stars
___ 2. Day two	b. Day and night
___ 3. Day three	c. Birds and Fish
___ 4. Day four	d. Plants and trees
___ 5. Day five	e. Animals and man
___ 6. Day six	f. Sea and sky

Look on the next page for the answers…

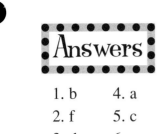

Answers

1. b   4. a
2. f   5. c
3. d   6. e

God created a perfect world, but then sin entered the world when Adam and Eve disobeyed God in the Garden of Eden. They had to leave the garden.

Adam and Eve's two oldest sons were named Cain and Abel. Cain committed the first murder. You can read about it for yourself.

Read It

Read Genesis 4:1-15 in your Bible. Then answer these questions.

What was Abel's job? (verse 2) _____

What was Cain's job? (verse 2) _____

What did Cain sacrifice to God? (verse 3) _____

What did Abel sacrifice to God? (verse 4) _____

The Bible doesn't say why God rejected Cain's offering. How did Cain feel when God did not accept his offering? (verse 5) _____

_____

Cain was jealous and angry that Abel's sacrifice was accepted. What did he do about his feelings? (verse 8) _____

_____

How did God punish him? (verse 12) _____

_____

How did God promise to protect him? (verse 15) _____

_____

What could Cain have done differently when God rejected his offering?

_____

_____

Like Cain, have you ever been jealous of someone? What did you do about it?

_____

_____

What are some good things to do about jealousy?

_____

_____

The Flood (Genesis 6:1–8:22)

People got more wicked as time went by. Finally, God decided to destroy the world through a flood.

God told Noah to build an ark. This wasn't just a weekend job. It took Noah 120 years to build it! It had to be big enough for Noah's family, the animals and food for everyone. The ark was 450 feet long, 75 feet wide, and 45 feet high.

Turn the page for a crossword puzzle that will teach you more about Noah.

Did You Know?

The Bible contains hundreds of predictions made in Bible times that have already come true!

☞ Do It

Use the word list to solve the clues, then write the correct word in the puzzle on the next page. The solution is on page 191.

Word List

altar	covenant	cypress
destroy	dove	forty
Ham	Japheth	mountains
olive leaf	rainbow	raven
Shem	six hundred	three (use this word twice)

Across

1. God set this in the clouds as a sign of His covenant with Noah.

5. One of Noah's sons.

7. Noah sent out the dove this many times.

8. God made a _____ with Noah.

9. The kind of wood Noah used to build the ark.

12. One of Noah's sons.

14. The water even covered these.

15. The second kind of bird Noah sent from the ark.

Down

2. Noah built one of these to God.

3. The first kind of bird Noah sent from the ark.

4. God said he would do this to the earth because of the wickedness.

6. Number of days it rained.

7. Number of decks on the ark.

10. Age Noah was when he entered the ark.

11. One of Noah's sons.

13. What the dove brought to Noah.

The Tower of Babel (Genesis 11:1-8)

Hannah sat at the cafeteria table eating her lunch. She was mumbling something under her breath.

"Hannah, what are you saying?" Melissa asked. "It sounds like mumbo jumbo. How are we suppose to talk to you if we can't understand you?"

"Oh, I started Spanish club after school last night. We are going to learn a little Spanish each week so that we can decide if we want to take Spanish in high school. It was kind of fun really."

"I didn't know about it," Melissa said.

"Me neither," Amber said. "Is it too late to join? Maybe Melissa and I could start coming to Spanish club, too. Then we could talk to each other in Spanish."

"Yeah, it could be like a secret language or something," Melissa said.

"Cool idea. It's probably not too late to start, and I can teach you what we learned last night," Hannah said. "Let's start now!"

Do you speak more than one language? What do you speak?

_____

Have you ever been in an airport or another place where a lot of people were speaking different languages? How did it feel to have people around you speaking words that you couldn't understand?

_____

_____

After the flood, people spread out over the earth, but they all spoke the same language. Some people decided that they would build a tower that reached to heaven as a way of making themselves seem as important as God. But as they were building their tower, God gave them all new languages. Suddenly they couldn't understand each other! Imagine how hard it would be to finish a tower together if you don't speak the same language.

How do you think the people felt when all of a sudden they couldn't understand each other?

_____

_____

Abraham (Genesis 12:1–13:18)

"But I don't want to move," Carrie yelled. She went into her room and banged the door. Then she quietly opened it and listened for a reaction. Hearing none, she slammed shut the door louder just to make sure her parents heard it.

"How can they expect me to be happy about moving?" she asked herself. All my friends are here. I just made the gymnastics team and I start competing in a couple of months. And I'm really, really looking forward to going to church camp again this year. How can they do this to me?

Carrie didn't know whether to scream, cry, or hit her pillow! She felt like doing all of them.

If you've ever had to move, what was the hardest part?

_____

How did you make new friends?

_____

_____

What was the best part about moving?

_____

In Genesis chapter 12, God calls Abraham to leave his country and people to follow Him. Abraham not only had to leave his home, he didn't even know where he was going! Abraham obeyed God and God made some promises to Abraham. He promised to bless Abraham, to make him the father of a great nation and to bless the children and all generations after them.

When God made these promises to Abraham, Abraham and Sarah didn't have any children. They wondered if God had made a mistake! How could He bless their family and make a great nation from them when they didn't have children? But when Abraham was 100 years old and Sarah was 90, God gave them a son. They named him Isaac. Then God asked Abraham to do something really hard. You can read about it for yourself.

 # Read It

Read Genesis 22:1-19 in your Bible. Then answer the questions.

What did God ask Abraham to do? (verse 2)

_____

How did Abraham get there? (verse 3)

_____

How many days did they travel? (verse 4) _____

What did Isaac ask his father? (verse 7)

_____

_____

How do you think Isaac felt when he realized he was going to be the sacrifice?

_____

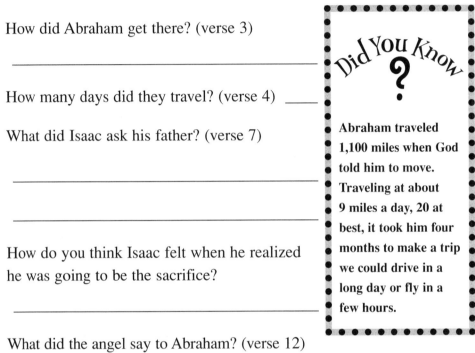

Did You Know?

Abraham traveled 1,100 miles when God told him to move. Traveling at about 9 miles a day, 20 at best, it took him four months to make a trip we could drive in a long day or fly in a few hours.

What did the angel say to Abraham? (verse 12)

_____

_____

What did Abraham sacrifice? (verse 13) _____

How might this story have been different if Abraham wasn't willing to obey God?

_____

_____

Write about a time when it was hard for you to obey God.

_____

_____

Like Abraham, would you be willing to give up the most precious thing in your life for God?

_____

_____

Jacob and Esau (Genesis 25:19–35:29)

When Abraham and Sarah's son, Isaac, was grown, God sent him a wife named Rebekah. Isaac and Rebekah had twin boys named Jacob and Esau. Jacob's name means "to cheat." When you read Genesis, you see that he lived up to his name! He tricked his older brother, Esau, out of his birthright (extra privileges and possessions that the oldest son was to receive). Then he tricked his father into giving him a blessing intended for Esau. Esau was so angry with Jacob that Jacob ran away to his Uncle Laban's house.

☞ Do It

What did Jacob give Esau in exchange for his birthright? Use the clocks on the next page to help you find out.

_____   _____

12:00   1:00 6:00 9:00 4:00

_____   _____

6:00 3:00   7:00 10:00 11:00 9:00

37

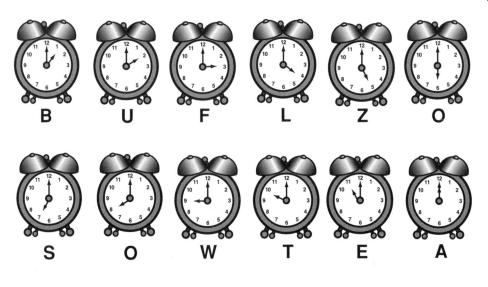

B	U	F	L	Z	O

S	O	W	T	E	A

Answer: A bowl of stew.

At Laban's house, Jacob the trickster had a trick played on him! Laban had two daughters, Leah and Rachel. Jacob loved Rachel and worked seven years to be allowed to marry her. But when the time came, he found himself married to Leah instead because Laban had tricked him into marrying her. Jacob had to work another seven years for Rachel! (Men had more than one wife in Bible times.)

Jacob learned to listen more to God. God honored his work by changing his name to Israel, which means "Prince of God."

Joseph (Genesis 37–46)

Jacob had 12 sons and a daughter. His youngest two sons, Joseph and Benjamin, were his favorites because their mother was Rachel, and she was his favorite wife.

☞ Do It

Do the crossword puzzle to find out more about Joseph. The solution is on page 191.

Word List

Benjamin	Canaan	cisterns
cows	cupbearer	Dinah
donkeys	eleven	famine
Goshen	grain	household
Ishmaelites	Pharaoh	Potiphar
prison	seventeen	shechem
Simeon	slave	spies
thirty	twenty	

Across

2. Joseph sent 10 of these loaded with gifts (45:23).
4. Seven of these came out of the river in a dream (41:2).
5. Where the brothers had gone with the flocks (37:12).
9. The seven worthless heads of grain stood for this (41:27).
13. Joseph was this old when he started serving Pharaoh (41:46).
14. Joseph was this old when he helped with the flocks (37:2).
15. These people were traveling in a caravan (37:25).
17. Joseph's master put him here after his wife lied about Joseph (39:20).
20. Joseph said this brother must come with the other brothers to get grain (43:14).
21. Joseph's father was here (45:25).
22. The man with the cup would become Joseph's _____ (44:17).

Down

1. One of the men in prison (39:20).
2. Joseph's sister (46:15).
3. Joseph was in charge of the whole _____ (39:5).

6. The number of stars that bowed to Joseph in his dream (37:7).

7. Joseph had a dream about sheaves of this (37:7).

8. The brothers threw Joseph into one of the _____ (37:20).

10. The brothers sold Joseph for this many shekels of silver (37:28).

11. Joseph was sold to one of Pharaoh's servants named this (37:36).

12. He put Joseph in charge of all the land (41:41).

16. Joseph had this brother bound (42:24).

18. Joseph accused the brothers of being these (42:9).

19. Joseph's family moved to this land (45:10).

Make It

Shirt of Many Colors

Joseph was his dad's favorite. Because of this, Jacob gave Joseph a colorful robe. In Bible stories it is often called his "coat of many colors." Make this colorful shirt to remind you of how Joseph stood up for what was right.

This project requires an adult's help. Work in the sink area to avoid dripping dye and staining surfaces.

What You Need

* white T-shirt
* rubber bands
* newspaper
* yellow and pink fabric dye
* two large pans or buckets
* old towels

What to Do

1. Cover your work area with newspaper.
2. Accordion fold (like you are making a fan) the T-shirt from the bottom edge diagonally to the top.
3. Wrap four or five rubber bands evenly-spaced around the T-shirt. Double them to make them tight. (This will make white or light colored lines in your pattern.)
4. Have an adult help you mix pink dye in one container and yellow in the other according to the directions on the box or bottle.
5. Submerge half the shirt in the yellow dye and hold it in place for seven minutes, then remove it.
6. Dip the other half in the pink dye for seven minutes (less for a lighter pink). Where the yellow and the pink overlap you will have orange!
7. Rinse the shirt–one color at a time–in cold water until the water runs clear.
8. Roll the shirt in an old towel and squeeze out the excess water.
9. Remove the rubber bands.
10. Finish drying the shirt in a clothes dryer.

☞ Do It

Even after Joseph suffered unfairly more than once, he could see that it was all part of God's plan. Use the code below to read what Joseph said. Decoding the message is easy. If you read A2, put one finger on the A and one on the 2. Trace the A across and the 2 down until your fingers meet. The A2 becomes Y.

	1	2	3	4	5	6
	A	Y	B	X	C	W
	T	F	U	E	V	D
	G	S	H	J	I	R
	P	O	N	M	L	K

_____   _____   _____

A2 P2 T3   G5 P3 T1 T4 P3 T6 T4 T6   T1 P2

_____   _____   _____   _____

G3 A1 G6 P4   P4 T4   A3 T3 T1   G1 P2 T6

_____   _____   _____

G5 P3 T1 T4 P3 T6 T4 T6   G5 T1   T2 P2 G6

_____

G1 P2 P2 T6

Memorize this verse so when bad things happen or it seems nothing is going right you remember God can use it to accomplish something good!

God led Abraham to Canaan. His family lived there until they moved to Egypt. In the next section you will read about how the Israelites made their way back from Egypt to Canaan, the land God promised His people.

Answer:
"You intended to harm me, but God intended it for good." (Genesis 50:20)

Exodus

The book of Genesis ends with Joseph's family moving to Egypt. The book of Exodus starts about 400 years later. In that time, Joseph's family grew from 70 people to millions! There were now millions of Israelites living in Egypt.

Moses
(Exodus 2:1–7:13)

The pharaoh in Egypt saw all the Israelites and worried that there were so many of them that they could make war against him. He decided to make their lives difficult so they would leave or die. But they stayed, so he made them slaves who had to

make bricks and build cities in the hot sun. And then he made a really bad rule. You can read about it for yourself.

 Read It

Read Exodus 1:22 and 2:1-15 in your Bible. Then answer the questions.

What order did Pharaoh give? (1:22)

_____

What did Moses' mother do when he was born? (verse 2)

_____

What did she do when this didn't work any longer? (verse 3)

_____

Who found Moses? (verse 5) _____

43

What did Miriam do? (verses 7-8)   _____

Where did Moses go to live when he was older? (verse 10)

_____

When Moses was 40, he left there. Why? (verses 11-12)

_____

Where did he go? (verse 15)   _____

Did Moses' mother's plan work?_____

Sometimes God uses the bad things that happen to people to make good things happen. Think of something that happened to you that seemed bad at the time but good came of it. (For example, maybe you had to move and leave all your friends but then you found a really good Christian friend at your new school.)

_____

_____

M oses lived as the son of Pharaoh's daughter. He was educated and had everything he needed. After 40 years he fled and became a shepherd in Midian. Then God spoke to Moses and told him to go to Pharaoh and tell him, "Let my people go." God wanted Moses to lead the Israelites from slavery.

Moses didn't want to go to Pharaoh, but when God said Moses' brother Aaron could go with him, Moses agreed to go. But the pharaoh wouldn't let the people go as Moses asked, so God made 10 bad things happen. These are called the plagues.

You can read about the ten plagues in Exodus 7:14-12:33, but here's a quick review of what happened:

※ The Nile River turned to blood. All the fish died, and the people didn't have any water.

※ Frogs covered the whole country. They came up from the water and completely covered the land.

※ The ground dust turned into gnats. People weren't just swatting them out of their eyes. Gnats were everywhere!

※ The houses and land were filled with flies. Imagine trying to sleep with thousands of flies in your bedroom!

※ All of the Egyptians' livestock died: horses, donkeys, camel, cattle, sheep and goats.

※ Moses took handfuls of ashes and threw them into the air, then horrible sores called boils broke out on all of the Egyptians.

※ Hail fell and killed every unprotected person, animal and most of the crops.

※ Locusts arrived and ate everything left after the hailstorm including trees.

※ Total darkness covered the land for three days. No one could see to do anything.

※ The first born of all people and animals died.

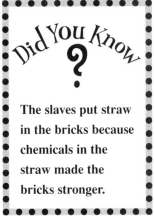

Did You Know?

The slaves put straw in the bricks because chemicals in the straw made the bricks stronger.

Finally after living in frog-filled, gnat-filled, locust-filled houses…and after being in the dark and having no water…and after being covered in painful boils and losing all the animals, crops, and firstborn children, Pharaoh decided to let the Israelites go free.

Pretend you are a newspaper reporter in Egypt during the plagues. Write a newspaper story below that tells about one or all of the plagues.

The Egyptian Times 1446 BC

Strange things have been taking place in Egypt lately...

_____

_____

_____

_____

The Israelites Prepare to Leave (Exodus 12:31–14:31)

Jessica looked around the house. What a mess! Packing boxes were everywhere. Some were already neatly sealed and had the contents listed on the side. Other boxes were half-full.

Jessica wanted to sit down, but her bed was covered with clothes waiting to be packed. "I hate moving!" she exclaimed.

Even though she hated to move, Jessica moved seven times while her dad was in the military. Each move meant cleaning out unwanted stuff and getting the rest ready to pack. It took two days to box up all the household goods each time. And then it all had to be unpacked at the other end!

Can you imagine what it was like for millions of Israelites to pack up and leave? God led the Egyptians to give the Israelites articles of silver and gold, and clothing. Since the Israelites'

animals weren't harmed in the plagues there were not only millions of people getting ready to move, there were large herds of animals also. It was probably a very loud and confusing time!

What do you think it would have been like to be among the children getting ready to leave Egypt?

_____

_____

After Pharaoh let the Israelites go, he regretted his decision. He sent his army to chase after them and bring them back. The Israelites had the Red Sea in front of them, and the Egyptians chasing them from behind. Read for yourself what happened.

 Read It

Read Exodus 14 in your Bible. If you can't read it all at one time, read 10 verses one day, 10 verses the next day and 11 verses the next day. Then answer the questions below.

Why was Pharaoh sorry he let the Israelites go? (verse 5)

_____

How did he plan to get them back? (verses 6-7)

_____

How did the Israelites feel when they saw them coming? (verse 10)

_____

What did God tell Moses to do? (verse 16)

_____

What happened? (verse 21)

_____

What happened when the Egyptians reached the sea? (verses 27-28)

_____

_____

This is just one of the ways that God took care of His people. Write about a time when you needed help and God took care of you.

_____

_____

_____

_____

The Israelites were finally free! But it didn't take them long to start complaining about eating manna (a bread that God sent each day) and not having enough water and other things. Sometimes they forgot to thank God for taking care of them. Sometimes we do the same thing!

☞ Do It

Where did Moses get water for the people? Cross out the first letter, then write the second letter on the line and so on to find out.

A F O R W O N M D A S R P O K C E K

_____

_____

The Ten Commandments (Exodus 20:3-17)

After they had been traveling a few months, the people arrived at Mount Sinai. This was the same place where God had spoken to Moses in the burning bush. This time, God talked to Moses and gave him some rules for the people. We call these "the Ten Commandments."

You can read the Ten Commandments in Exodus 20:3-17. The language might seem a bit old, so here is what the commandments mean to us today:

I. YOU SHALL HAVE NO GODS BEFORE ME.

II. YOU SHALL NOT MAKE FOR YOURSELF A GRAVEN IMAGE.

III. YOU SHALL NOT TAKE THE NAME OF THE LORD YOUR GOD IN VAIN.

IV. REMEMBER THE SABBATH DAY, TO KEEP IT HOLY.

V. HONOR YOUR FATHER AND YOUR MOTHER.

VI. YOU SHALL NOT KILL.

VII. YOU SHALL NOT COMMIT ADULTERY.

VIII. YOU SHALL NOT STEAL.

IX. YOU SHALL NOT BEAR FALSE WITNESS AGAINST YOUR NEIGHBOR.

X. YOU SHALL NOT COVET.

 Don't let anything be more important to you than God. Don't love anyone more than God.

 Don't make anyone (friends, parents, movie stars, athletes) be more special to you than God.

 Do not use God's name as a swear word. Use it only to talk about God.

 One day of the week should be set apart to worship God.

 Respect your parents.

 Do not hurt or harm another person.

 Be pure in your thoughts and actions. When you marry, be faithful to that person.

 Do not take something that belongs to someone else.

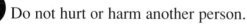 Do not lie or tell lies that will hurt another person.

Do not be jealous of what other people have.

Even though these laws were given to Moses and the Israelites, they are still important rules to follow. The first four rules talk about your relationship with God. The next six talk about your relationship with other people.

Moses was gone a long time while God gave him the Ten Commandments. The Israelites thought he wasn't coming back. Read for yourself what they did.

 # Read It

Read Exodus 32:1-20 in your Bible. Then answer the questions.

What did the Israelites ask Aaron to do? (verse 1)

_____

What did Aaron tell the people to give him? (verse 2)

_____

What did Aaron make? (verse 4)

_____

What did the people do with it? (verse 6)

_____

What did Moses do when he saw them? (verses 19-20)

_____

The Israelites built a real idol. Sometimes we turn things in our lives into idols by making them more important than God. What is something that could become more important to you than God?

_____

How can you keep God the most important thing to you?

_____

God told Moses to build a special place for the people to worship. Usually people worshipped in a stone building called a temple. But there weren't any temples as they traveled in the wilderness. So Moses built a tabernacle that could be set up for worship. It was like a portable church! Inside the tabernacle was a special box called the Ark of the Covenant. It held the stone tablets on which the Ten Commandments were written.

When the people set up the tabernacle, a cloud came over it. When God wanted the people to travel, the cloud lifted. When they were not supposed to travel, the cloud stayed over the tabernacle. The cloud was like a traffic light!

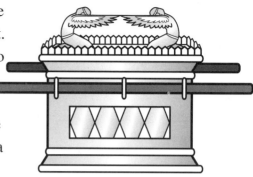

Leviticus

"Leviticus" means "about the Levites." The Levites were the priests and worship leaders. Leviticus doesn't tell a story. It contains rules especially for the priests and some rules for all of the Israelites.

Leviticus 1:1–7:21 tells about different offerings or sacrifices the people made to God. Here are some of them:

❋ Burnt offering–an animal or bird given to symbolize commitment to God or to make up for a sin that wasn't committed on purpose.

❋ Grain or meal offering– grain or bread with olive oil that symbolized devotion to God.

❋ Fellowship or peace offering–a perfect animal symbolizing thanksgiving.

❋ Sin offering–an animal based on what the offender could provide to make up for his sin.

❋ Guilt offering–a valuable ram or lamb given to atone for sins or for cleansing of guilt.

We don't have to offer sacrifices. Jesus died on the cross to pay the penalty for our sins. Now we can confess our sins and ask God to forgive us and He will because of what Jesus did for us.

Leviticus also lists many feasts and festivals for all occasions including rest for people, rest for the land, remembrance of the Israelites' deliverance from Egypt, recognition of thankfulness and other special times and seasons.

What special occasions does your family celebrate and how do you celebrate them?

_____

_____

Numbers

The book of Numbers starts with a census taken at Sinai. A census is a formal count of all the people in a land. Moses may have counted them so he would know how many men there were to fight against the enemy. He may have also counted them so he could give each group of people enough land when they reached the Promised Land. The Promised Land was the land to which God was leading them after Egypt.

The groups of people were called tribes. Each of Jacob's sons and all of the sons' relatives made up a tribe. Here are the names of the tribes:

Reuben	Simeon	Judah
Issachar	Dan	Zebulun
Benjamin	Naphtali	Asher
Gad	Ephraim	Manasseh

Did you notice that Joseph isn't listed? He's not, but the last two listed–Ephraim and Manasseh–are his sons, so really there are two tribes representing Joseph. There is no Levi tribe either because the Levites were priests and they would live among the other tribes to help them obey and worship God.

After the count, the Israelites were ready to move from Mount Sinai to Canaan, the Promised Land. But the Israelites were grumbling again! They even said it would be better to be slaves again than to continue eating manna and living in the wilderness. They forgot how it felt to be a slave! More importantly, they forgot how God had taken care of them and that He had a plan for them.

When the Israelites finally reached the border of Canaan, they simply had to go in and conquer the land. Did they do it? Read it for yourself.

 # Read It

You will be reading several different passages.

Read Numbers 13:1-2 What did God tell Moses to have some men do?

_____

Read Numbers 13:27-28. What was the good news the men gave Moses?

_____

What was the bad news?

_____

Read Numbers 13:30-33. What did Caleb say they should do?

_____

What did the others say?

_____

Read Numbers 14:6-10. What did Caleb and Joshua tell the people?

_____

What did the people threaten to do to Caleb and Joshua?

_____

Read Numbers 14:28-34. How did God punish the people for not trusting and obeying Him?

_____

What are some times when it is hard for you to obey God?

_____

Remember that when God asks you to do something, He will help you do it!

The Spies Sent Out (Numbers 13:1–14:38)

The people were still complaining. They were ready to give up! When 10 of 12 men sent to check the Promised Land said they would not be able to conquer it, they even said they wished they had died in Egypt. They wouldn't listen to Caleb and Joshua. They wouldn't obey God.

God was not happy with the Israelites, so He made them wander around the wilderness for 40 more years! (That was one year for each day that the men spied on the land.) All of the adults died without ever entering the Promised Land. Only Caleb and Joshua entered it. They paid the price for refusing to trust God and take the land He provided!

The map at the top of the next page shows the route the Israelites took through the desert. Can you draw the faster route they could have traveled if they had trusted God?

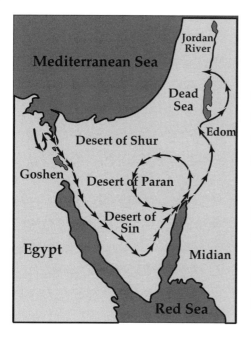

Balaam and His Donkey
(Numbers 22:21–41)

During the rest of the book of Numbers, the Israelites wander and fight against various groups of people. When they listened to God, they defeated their enemies.

The king of Moab became frightened and sent for a man named Balaam. He wanted Balaam to put a curse on the Israelites. But God told Balaam to do only what He said to do.

The next morning, Balaam got on his donkey and started off to see the king of Moab. God sent an angel to block his way. The donkey saw the angel standing in the way holding a sword, but Balaam didn't see it. Balaam tried beating his donkey to get it to move, but the donkey wouldn't budge.

Then the Lord allowed the donkey to speak. It said, "What have I done to you to make you beat me these three times?"

Balaam answered, "You have made a fool of me! If I had a sword in my hand, I would kill you right now."

Then the Lord let Balaam see the angel, too. Balaam fell face down. Afterward he went on his way but when he reached the Israelites, instead of cursing them, God would only allow him to bless them!

Deuteronomy

After 40 years, the Israelites who had only been children when the journey to the Promised Land began were now adults ready to enter the land. In Deuteronomy, Moses reminds them of God's help in the past and of God's laws. Deuteronomy means "second law."

Moses was now 120 years old. Do you remember how he spent his life? His life was divided into three 40-year periods.

During his first 40 years Moses lived briefly with his family and then was raised by _____.

During his next 40 years, Moses was a _____ in the land of _____.

During his last 40 years, Moses and the Israelites

_____.

Moses' life and work was now done. He died just before the people entered Canaan.

☞ Do It

Moses told the people many important things. Use the phone on the next page to help you decode the message so you can find out one of the things Moses told the people. The first number refers to the number on the phone dial. So 2 would mean #2 on the phone. Since #2 on the phone dial has three letters: a, b, c, a second number is given. The second number tells you which letter to use. For example 2.3 would mean #2 on the dial, then the third (3) letter, which is c.

This is a good verse to memorize and always remember.

5.3 6.3 8.3 3.2	8.1 4.2 3.2	5.3 6.3 7.2 3.1	9.3 6.3 8.2 7.2

—————   —————   —————   —————

4.1 6.3 3.1   9.1 4.3 8.1 4.2   2.1 5.3 5.3   9.3 6.3 8.2 7.2

—————   —————   —————   —————

4.2 3.2 2.1 7.2 8.1   2.1 6.2 3.1   9.1 4.3 8.1 4.2   2.1 5.3 5.3

—————   —————   —————   —————

9.3 6.3 8.2 7.2   7.3 6.3 8.2 5.3   2.1 6.2 3.1   9.1 4.3 8.1 4.2

—————   —————   ————————————

2.1 5.3 5.3   9.3 6.3 8.2 7.2   7.3 8.1 7.2 3.2 6.2 4.1 8.1 4.2

Answer: Love the Lord your God with all your heart and with all your soul and with all your strength. (Deuteronomy 6:5).

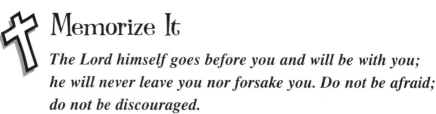

Memorize It

The Lord himself goes before you and will be with you; he will never leave you nor forsake you. Do not be afraid; do not be discouraged.

~ Deuteronomy 31:8

Chapter Three

Heroes in History

There are 12 history books. Each of the 12 books tells a part of Israel's story. These books are filled with action and drama! You'll read about Ehud, who smuggled a sword into King Eglon's own palace and killed him. You'll learn of Ruth, who knew the man she wanted to marry and how she told him she wanted to marry him. You'll meet Esther, who foiled Haman's plot to kill the Jews. And you'll read about many more people, both villains and heroes.

Joshua

The book of Joshua doesn't say who wrote it. Many people believe that Joshua wrote most of it himself. Joshua was one of the two spies who said that the Israelites should go into Canaan and conquer the people. But because the Israelites listened to the other spies, they had to wander in the wilderness for 40 years.

The book of Joshua starts with the younger generation of Israelites, who were willing to trust God, conquering Canaan. Moses died and Joshua became the leader.

The Lord gave Joshua many things to remember. God promised Joshua that He would always be with him.

Memorize It

Have I not commanded you? Be strong and courageous. Do not be terrified; do not be discouraged, for the Lord your God will be with you wherever you go.
~Joshua 1:9

Crossing the River (Joshua 3:1-17)

Joshua sent spies into the Promised Land while he and the people were camped on the other side of the Jordan River. The spies said the Israelites could conquer the land with God's help. But first, the people had to cross the Jordan River.

The priest who carried the Ark of the Covenant (the fancy box that held the Ten Commandments) stepped into the water and the river stopped flowing. The priest stood in the middle of the riverbed as the people crossed on land. As soon as everyone crossed, the priest stepped onto the dry ground. The river once again flooded its banks.

The Israelites had to fight battles with several different groups of people. Three cities they fought teach valuable lessons: Jericho, Ai and Gibeon.

The Walls of Jericho (Joshua 6:1-27)

To enter the land of Canaan, the Israelites had to go through Jericho. Jericho had high stone walls around it. It was almost impossible to get into Jericho to defeat it.

☞ Do It

Do the crossword puzzle on the next page to find out how Joshua and his men defeated Jericho. Use the Word List below. The solution is on page 191.

Word List

burned	covenant	Joshua	Rahab
sandals	seven	shout	six
sword	treasury	trumpets	

Across

3. All the silver and gold and bronze were to go in the Lord's

   _____ .

4. The priests carried the Ark of the _____ as they marched around the city.

7. All the people and animals were destroyed by this.

8. Number of times the people marched around the city on the seventh day.

9. Only she and her family were spared because she hid the spies and believed God.

10. Number of days they marched around the city once.

Down

1. They _____ the whole city after destroying all the living things.

2. God's chosen leader.

5. The priest blew these.

6. Joshua told the people to give a loud _____ and the walls fell.

7. Joshua was told to remove these because he was on holy ground.

Achan's Sin (Joshua 7:1-26)

The defeat of Jericho showed God's mighty power. But at Ai, which should have been an easy victory, the Israelites were defeated. You can read about it for yourself.

Read It

Read Joshua 7:1-25 and then answer the questions below.

How many men went to fight against the small city of Ai? (verse 4)

_____

Did they have the easy victory they expected? What happened? (verse 4)

_____

What did God say the Israelites had done wrong? (verse 11)

_____

How were the people to find out who sinned? (verse 14)

_____

What did Achan confess? (verse 20)

_____

What happened to Achan and his whole family because of his sin? (verse 25)

_____

Disobeying God cost Achan and his family their lives. It's important to obey God but sometimes we do sin. What should we do when we sin? (1 John 1:9)

_____

Gibeon (Joshua 9:1-27)

After Achan was killed, God let the Israelites defeat Ai. The people of Gibeon heard about it and were afraid. They decided to trick the Israelites, so they made their supplies and clothes look old and tattered. Then they told Joshua they had traveled a long distance and wanted to make a peace treaty with him.

Joshua was not supposed to make treaties with nations living near him, but he could make treaties with those from places farther away. Joshua fell for the Gibeonites' trick and he made a treaty with them without consulting God first. That was a big mistake! Later, Joshua found out the Gibeonites lived close to him, but he couldn't defeat them because of the treaty.

The cities of Jericho, Ai and Gibeon teach us three really important things about God:

1 Jericho shows us that when we obey God, we are victorious.

2 Ai demonstrates that when we disobey God we face consequences.

3 Gibeon teaches us that we should not make important decisions without talking to God first.

The rest of the book of Joshua talks about other battles the Israelites fought. Finally, each tribe was given land to settle. Families within the tribes were given their own piece of land within that land.

 # Make It

Wall Hanging

Before Joshua died (at the age of 110!) he gave the people an important challenge. He said to "fear the Lord and serve him with all faithfulness," (Joshua 24:14). This is a craft to help you remember to serve God with faithfulness. Turn the page for the instructions!

What You Need

✳ plain cloth, burlap or felt
✳ dowel rod
✳ fabric markers or fabric paint
✳ decorations (sequins, glitter, felt pieces, buttons or other small items)
✳ glue
✳ 18" of yarn
✳ pencil

What to Do

1. Cut your fabric to the size you want your banner. Your dowel rod should be 2" longer than the width of the fabric.
2. Lightly pencil the words "Serve the Lord Faithfully" on your banner. (This is a paraphrase of the verse. If you like, copy the whole verse from above.)
3. Once you have the words the way you want them to look, go over them in marker or paint.
4. Glue your decorations to the banner.
5. Allow to dry overnight.
6. Fold over 1" of the cloth to the back.
7. Glue down just the very edge of the cloth. Allow to dry thoroughly.
8. Slide the dowel rod through the 1" fold.
9. Tie the yarn to each end of the dowel rod.
10. Hang your banner in your room to remind you to serve the Lord.

Judges (The author of Judges is unknown.)

Rachel sat on the porch watching her little brother, Ryan, ride his tricycle. "Stay on the sidewalk," she called. "You'll get stuck if you go off the sidewalk into the mud."

For a while, Ryan happily rode his trike up and down the sidewalk. But then he decided to ride it across the yard. Shortly after he pedaled onto the grass, his wheels sunk into the soft mud and he was stuck. He tried rocking his trike forward and backward, but that only made it worse.

"Rachel, help me. I'm stuck," Ryan yelled.

"Okay, but I told you this would happen," Rachel said as she walked over to Ryan.

Rachel pulled Ryan back onto the sidewalk. "I'm going inside to call a friend," she said. "Stay on the sidewalk or you'll get stuck again."

Ryan stayed on the sidewalk for a few minutes. Then he rode off into the lawn again and got stuck.

"Rachel, Mommy, somebody help me," he yelled. "I'm stuck again."

In the book of Judges, the Israelites were something like Ryan. They disobeyed God, then other nations defeated and ruled them. The Israelites asked God to help them, and God sent someone to deliver them. Then it started all over again with the Israelites disobeying God.

In the book of Joshua, the people obeyed God and were victorious. In the book of Judges they did not obey God. They did not drive all of the people out of their land like they were supposed to do. God said to kill ALL the enemies–even women and children, but the Israelites did not do it. Some of them spared the women and children. Others kept some of the enemy alive and make them slaves. At times, the Israelites worshipped idols instead of God.

God sent 12 different people to deliver Israel. These people were called judges. The stories about the judges are full of action and adventure. One judge had a victory because he was left-handed. Another judge won a war with jars. One of the judges killed himself in order to kill his enemy, too. For a few judges, the Bible gives us very little information but their lives were probably just as interesting!

☞ Do It

See if you can match the judge with the correct description. Use the Bible references to help you.

_____ 1. Othneil (Judges 3:7-11)

_____ 2. Ehud (Judges 3:12-30)

_____ 3. Shamgar (Judges 3:31)

_____ 4. Deborah (Judges 4-5)

_____ 5. Gideon (Judges 6-8)

_____ 6. Tola (Judges 10:1)

_____ 7. Jair (Judges 10:3-5)

_____ 8. Jephthah (Judges 10:6-12:7)

_____ 9. Izban (Judges 12:8-9)

_____ 10. Elan (Judges 12:11-12)

_____ 11. Adbon (Judges 12:13-15)

_____ 12. Samson (Judges 13-16)

a. He was a left-handed judge. He wore his sword on his right side. The guards didn't check there and he was able to get his sword past the guards and kill Eglon. Eglon was so fat that the fat closed over the sword!

b. Barak and his 10,000 soldiers were supposed to go to battle against the Canaanites. He said he would only go if this judge went with him.

c. This judge had 30 sons who rode 30 donkeys and controlled 30 towns of Gilead.

d. He was from Bethlehem and had 30 sons and 30 daughters.

e. He killed 600 Philistines with an oxgoad–a common piece of farm equipment.

f. All we know about this judge is that he was a Zebulunite who led Israel for 10 years.

g. This judge asked for a sign from God before going to war against the Midianites. Then he took a very small army of only 300 men with unusual weapons–trumpets and jars–to defeat the Midianites.

h. Caleb's nephew. (Caleb was one of the spies who believed he could conquer the Promised Land). He went to war and defeated the king of Aram.

i. He had 40 sons and 30 grandsons who rode on 70 donkeys. He led Israel eight years.

j. This man was physically strong but morally weak. He let a girlfriend find out the secret of his strength and she betrayed him. In the end he died to save the Israelites.

k. All we know of this judge is that he was from the land of Shamir and led Israel for 23 years.

l. This judge vowed to God that if God let him be victorious then he would sacrifice whatever would come out of the door of his house to meet him. Instead of being the family pet, it was his beloved daughter.

Answers:
1. h   2. a   3. e   4. b   5. g   6. k
7. c   8. i   9. d   10. f   11. i   12. j

God Uses Ordinary People

Do you ever feel like the men and women in the Bible were all brave and mighty people and that you could never be like them? If so, guess again. God used some unlikely people to be His heroes in the book of Judges.

Ehud was one of God's chosen men (see Judges 3:12-30). Did he help Israel by being brave and noble? No. He helped Israel defeat a wicked king by being left-handed. He wore his sword on the right side–opposite of most soldiers. No one thought to check there. He was able to approach King Eglon, kill him with the sword, and leave before anyone discovered what he'd done.

Ehud used the way God created him to save his people.

Is there a way that you can use how God made you to be a hero to someone else? Here are some examples:

✳ If you are smart you could help a student who has trouble with her math homework.

✳ If you are friendly you could welcome new kids who visit your church.

✳ If you are strong you could help your teacher carry books to her car.

Write your idea here:

Shamgar was another judge. Most people have never heard of Shamgar because there is only one verse in the whole Bible about him, "After Ehud came Shamgar son of Anath, who struck down six hundred Philistines with an oxgoad. He too saved Israel" (Judges 3:31). An oxgoad? Not a sword or spear, but a common piece of farm equipment! Yet he was able to kill 600 of the enemy. Shamgar used something from everyday life to save the people of Israel.

Is there something around you that you could use to be a hero? Here are some examples:

✳ You could use a paintbrush to help paint the church nursery.

✳ You could use a mixer to make cookies for a busy mother.

✳ You could use markers to make a card for someone in a nursing home.

Write your idea here:

God chose Barak to fight the enemy, but Barak refused to go unless Deborah, a prophetess, went with him (see Judges 4:1-24). She told Barak that the glory for the victory would be the Lord's, not his, because Barak insisted that she go with him. Deborah, not Barak, was the judge. Deborah and Barak together saved God's people.

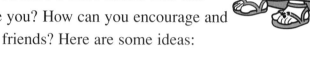

Do you have a close friend who can encourage you? How can you encourage and help your friends? Here are some ideas:

※ Help a friend clean her room when she's busy.
※ Offer to study for a test with a friend who has trouble with schoolwork.
※ Write a friend a note telling her what you like about her.

Write your idea here:

_____

When God called Gideon to fight a battle, he was hiding (see Judges 6:1–8:35). Gideon was afraid of the Midianites. If God had chosen a mighty warrior, that warrior would have claimed the victory for himself. But God used Gideon and a very small army so that He would get the glory.

Is there something that's hard for you to do? Could you use the Lord's help? Perhaps it's difficult for you to share your faith, or to befriend an unfriendly student. Write what you need God's help with:

_____

These are only a few of the unlikely heroes from the book of Judges. Read the book for yourself and see how God used unlikely heroes to deliver Israel from its enemies.

Ruth (The author of Ruth is unknown.)

The book of Ruth takes place during the time of the judges, but it doesn't talk about the Israelites. It is about Naomi, Ruth and Boaz. It's a story of courage and love.

There was a famine in Bethlehem. There was no food to eat and the people were hungry. Naomi and Elimelech and their two sons went to live in Moab. This wasn't a good place to go. Moab and Israel were enemies. Do you remember that Ehud (an Israelite) killed Eglon (the king of Moab)? And the people of Moab worshipped idols!

The two sons married women from Moab: Ruth and Orpah. Over time, the three men died. Naomi, Orpah and Ruth were all widows. Naomi heard the famine in Bethlehem had ended, so she decided to return to her homeland.

☞ Do It

What did Ruth tell Naomi she wanted to do? Write down the alphabet. Next, give each letter a number: A=1, B=2 and so on. Then write the letter that goes with each number on the line and read Ruth's message to Naomi.

_____ _____ ___ __ _____ ___
23 8 5 18 5   25 15 21   7 15   9   23 9 12 12   7 15,

___ _____ _____ _____ __
1 14 4   23 8 5 18 5   25 15 21   19 20 1 25   9

_____ _____. _____
23 9 12 12   19 20 1 25   25 15 21 18

_____ _____ __ ___
16 5 15 16 12 5   23 9 12 12   2 5   13 25

16	5	15	16	12	5		1	14	4		25	15	21	18		7	15	4

13 25   7 15 4.

Answer: Where you go I will go, and where you stay I will stay. Your people will be my people and your God my God. (Ruth 1:16)

Ruth and Naomi went to Naomi's homeland together. Naomi remembered that her husband had a relative named Boaz. Naomi told Ruth to go to Boaz's fields. When farmers harvested they left grain behind for the poor. Naomi wanted Ruth to go get the leftover grain for them to eat because neither Ruth nor Naomi had husbands or sons to care for them. When this happens they often marry a relative called a kinsman redeemer. Read for yourself how Boaz became a redeemer to Ruth.

 Read It

You can read all four short chapters of Ruth a bit at a time before answering the questions, or you can just read the verses given with each question to answer the questions.

How did Ruth meet Boaz? (Ruth 2:2-6)

_____

What did she ask Boaz? (Ruth 2:7)

_____

What did Boaz tell her? (Ruth 2:8)

_____

What did Ruth's mother-in-law tell her to do? (Ruth 3:1-4)

_____

Boaz told Ruth that there was a relative who was a closer relative to Elimelech's family than he was. That relative had the right to marry Ruth. Boaz would have to get permission from him to marry Ruth.

Did Boaz marry Ruth? (Ruth 4:1-10) _____

Ruth and Boaz had a son named Obed. He was the father of Jesse who was the father of the great King David. They were ancestors of Jesus.

1 & 2 Samuel (The author is unknown.)

The books of 1 & 2 Samuel, 1 & 2 Kings and 1 & 2 Chronicles overlap in telling about Samuel, Saul, David and Solomon.

Hannah's Son (1 Samuel 1:1–2:11)

1 Samuel begins with Hannah at the temple praying for a child. God answered her prayer and gave her Samuel, whose name means "asked of God." When Samuel was three, Hannah took him to the tabernacle and dedicated him to God's work. She had promised to do this if God answered her prayer for a child. Samuel served God by being a helper to Eli. Later, he served God as a priest, prophet and as Israel's last judge.

God had always ruled the Israelites with the help of the judges and other leaders He chose. Now they wanted a king. God said they had rejected Him as king. He had Samuel warn the Israelites that life would be different if they chose a person as a king over them. The people didn't listen.

The People Want a King (1 Samuel 8:1–10:27)

☞ Do It

Samuel anointed Saul as king. Where was Saul? Write the letter that comes after the letter given to find the answer.

_____   _____   _____   _____

G H C H M F   Z L N M F   S G D   A Z F F Z F D.

Answer: Hiding among the baggage (1 Samuel 10:22)

72

Saul was tall and strong. At first, Saul listened to Samuel and to God and was a good king. But then he stopped following Samuel's orders. Samuel told Saul that he would not rule long because he disobeyed God. God told Samuel to anoint a new king who would take over after Saul died. Who did Samuel choose? Read it for yourself.

 Read It

Read 1 Samuel 16:1-13 in your Bible. Then answer the questions below.

To what town did God send Samuel? (verse 1)

_____

Why was Samuel concerned? (verse 2)

_____

Who did Samuel think God was going to chose? (verse 6)

_____

Did God choose one of the older brothers? (verses 7-11)

_____

Who did God want to be the next king? (verse 13)

_____

Sometimes we judge people by how good looking or talented they are. Does God choose people the same way that we do? What does God look at? (verse 7)

_____

_____

How can we see people more like God sees them?

_____

Goliath the Giant (1 Samuel 17:1-58)

A giant named Goliath challenged the Israelites. He said that if anyone could kill him, the Philistines would serve the Israelites, but if he won, the Israelites would have to serve the Philistines. No one wanted to take him up on that challenge–except David, a boy. David took his sling and stones and faced Goliath. While Goliath was still mocking David, David let the rock fly from his sling. Whoosh! Down came the mighty Goliath!

Many more victories followed David's battle with Goliath. Whatever Saul asked David to do, he did it successfully with God's help. Soon the people were dancing and singing, "Saul has slain his thousands, and David his tens of thousands." They were saying that David was better than King Saul was. Do you think Saul was happy with this? No! He was very jealous. From that time, he decided to kill David.

Saul's son, Jonathan, didn't feel the same way. 1 Samuel 18 tells us that Jonathan loved David. Jonathan could have been jealous. He was next in line to be king, but God chose David instead. Jonathan wasn't jealous! He gave David special gifts: his own robe and tunic, and even his sword, bow and belt. Read about it in 1 Samuel 19:1–20:52.

Look on the next page for something you can make to give to your best friend!

Make It

Friendship Pins

Want to make an easy gift for your friends? Here is an idea that takes only a minute or two to make.

What You Need

* safety pins
* beads

What to Do

1. Open the safety pin and thread on as many beads as you can fit.

2. Make colorful patterns or choose your friends' favorite colors.

3. Make matching pins for yourself and your friends.

4. Fasten the pins to your shoelaces.

Saul's and Jonathan's deaths are both listed at the end of 1 Samuel. In 2 Samuel, David begins his reign as king. At first, David only ruled over the people of Judah (the southern tribes). Ish-bosheth, Saul's son ruled over the rest. Later, the other tribes asked David to be their king also.

One thing that David had to do was capture the city of Jerusalem. His soldiers got into the city by crawling up through a water shaft that went from the city into the valley. Once his soldiers had captured Jerusalem, David made it his capital city. He brought the Ark of the Covenant there and wanted to build a temple to put it in. God told David that he was not the one to build the temple. God said David's son would build it.

David's Sin (2 Samuel 11:1–12:25)

Even though David was a follower of God, he was human and he sinned. David met Bathsheba. She was married to another man, but she and David had a baby together. David had Bathsheba's husband killed to cover up their sin.

Nathan, a godly man, helped David see his sin. David confessed his sin and God forgave him, but He said that the baby would die. The baby did die, but David had other sons.

When David was old, one of his sons, Absalom, wanted to kill David so that he could be king. That made David very sad. Even some of David's men were in on the plot to kill David.

But God had other plans. Absalom had long hair. One day when he was trying to escape on a mule, the mule ran under a tree and Absalom's long hair got tangled in the tree. David's loyal men found Absalom and killed him.

There were many people who wanted to be the king after David. David appointed Solomon to be the next king. Solomon would also be the one to build the temple.

You will read about Solomon in 1 &2 Kings.

1 & 2 Kings

No author for Kings is named, but some people think it was the prophet Jeremiah.

Solomon Asks for Wisdom (1 Kings 3:1-15)

Solomon became king after David's death. One day, Solomon went to Gibeon to offer sacrifices. God appeared to Solomon and said, "Ask for whatever you want me to give you."

Wow! That's better than a genie in a bottle because we know that God always keeps His promises. What would you have asked for?

_____

Solomon knew it was going to be hard to be a good king. He knew there would be difficult decisions to make. Solomon asked for wisdom to rule the people and to know right from wrong. Because Solomon asked for wisdom instead of riches, God said he would not only give Solomon the wisdom he asked for but that he would give him riches AND honor .

Solomon was a wise king. One day, two mothers came to Solomon with a baby (see 1 Kings 3:26-28). Both claimed the baby was hers. Solomon pretended he would cut the baby in half. One mother stopped him and said to give the baby to the other mother rather than kill the baby. Solomon knew she was the real mother.

Solomon Builds the Temple (1 Kings 5–6)

Remember that God told David he couldn't build the temple but that his son would? Solomon did build the temple and it was a splendid temple built with only the finest materials. It took 30,000 men seven years to build the temple. When it was finished, the Ark of the Covenant was brought into it and there was a two-week celebration.

Solomon also built a palace for himself that took 13 years to create.

Solomon started out as a godly king, but later he turned away from God and worshipped idols. Because of that, Solomon's son would not be king over Solomon's entire kingdom. Rehoboam would only be king over the two tribes of Judah. These were the southern tribes.

One of Solomon's leaders, named Jeroboam, became king of the 10 tribes of Israel. These were the northern tribes.

Elijah (1 Kings 17:1–19:21)

In the following years both kingdoms had kings who followed God and kings who didn't. But King Ahab was one of the most wicked kings of Israel.

☞ Do It

Do the crossword puzzle to find out more about King Ahab and Queen Jezebel and the showdown between God and Baal. All of the references are from 1 Kings. The solution is on page 191.

Word List

afraid	altar	angel
black	bulls	Carmel
earthquake	Elisha	fire
forty	Jehu	Kishon
noon	sacrifice	sleeping
swords	three	whisper

Across

8. Elijah told Ahab to meet him on Mount _____. (18:19)
9. The prophets cut themselves with these. (18:28)
10. Elijah built this of stones. (18:32)
11. Elijah said that Baal might be doing this. (18:27)
13. Number of days Elijah traveled to Horeb. (19:8)
15. The sky turned this color. (18:45)
17. God told Elijah to anoint this person to be prophet after him. (19:16)
18. He told Elijah to eat. (19:7)

Down

1. Elijah was _____ and ran for his life. (19:3)
2. Elijah offered this to God. (18:36)
3. This fell from heaven. (18:38)
4. Two of these were used for sacrifices. (18:23)
5. Number of times the four jars were filled with water and poured on the altar. (18:34)

6. Valley where the prophets of Baal were killed. (18:40)
7. The prophets of Baal called on him from morning until _____ (18:26).
12. God was not in the wind, or fire, or this. (19:12)
14. God spoke to Elijah in this. (19:12)
16. God told Elijah to anoint him the next king. (19:16)

Ahab and Jezebel were both very wicked. God used the prophet Elijah to show them and all the people that God is the only God. Elijah showed God's power in defeating the prophets of Baal.

The prophet Elijah trained Elisha to take his place. Both were very godly men. 2 Kings starts with the ministries of Elijah and Elisha. You can read about them for yourself.

 # Read It

Read 2 Kings 2:1-18, then answer the questions below.

How was God going to take Elijah to heaven? (verse 1)

_____

Elijah went a lot of places on the day he was taken. Name the places he went. (verses 1, 2, 4, 6)

_____

Elijah asked Elisha what he could do for him before he was taken. For what did Elisha ask? (verse 9)

_____

What did Elijah tell Elisha had to happen for him to get his request? (verse 10)

_____

Did it happen? (verse 11-12)

_____

Some of the people didn't know what happened and searched for Elijah. How many men searched for how long? (verse 17)

_____

Solomon asked for wisdom and Elisha asked for a double portion of Elijah's spirit. He wanted to accomplish more for God. Both men asked for things that would help them serve God better. For what would you ask God that would help you live a better Christian life?

_____

Namaan Is Healed (2 Kings 5:1-27)

Namaan, a commander, came to Elisha to be healed. Here is how the story might have happened.

Namaan **Servant Girl** **Elisha**

Messenger **Jordan River**

was a great captain in the army. But was sad. He had a skin disease called leprosy. A who worked for told him to go see the prophet of God. could tell him how to be healed.

took his horses and chariot to the house of . But did not come out. He sent out a . The told , "Go wash in the 7 times and you will be healed."

was angry! He wanted to come out and heal him. did not want to wash in the 7 times. His servants told him to try it–maybe it would work! went to the

81

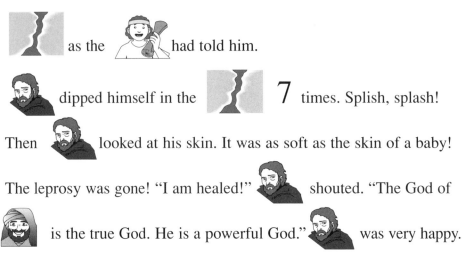 as the 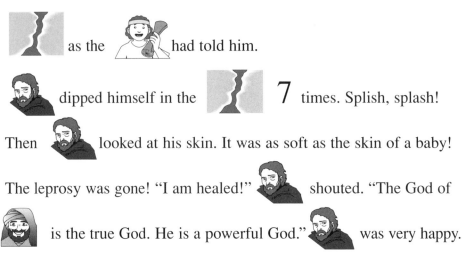 had told him.

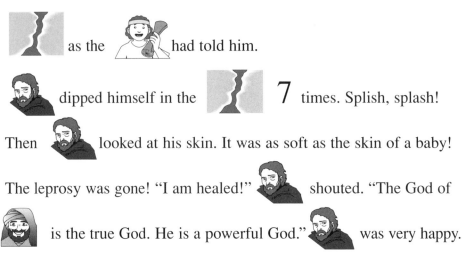 dipped himself in the 7 times. Splish, splash!

Then looked at his skin. It was as soft as the skin of a baby!

The leprosy was gone! "I am healed!" shouted. "The God of

 is the true God. He is a powerful God." was very happy.

The Northern Kingdom Is Captured (2 Kings 17:7-23)

Elisha did many miracles and also gave the people God's

messages. Sometimes the people didn't listen. God told Israel that if they listened, He would bless them. He told them that if they didn't obey Him, they would be sent out of the land. Israel did not obey God. The 10 northern tribes that made up Israel were captured by the Assyrians and taken to Assyria.

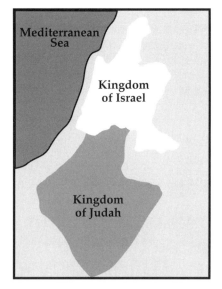

The Southern Kingdom Is Captured (2 Kings 24–25)

The Assyrians were mighty for 300 years until Babylonia became more powerful and conquered Assyria. Then they conquered Judah, the southern kingdom. The people were taken to Babylonia to live. God promised it would only be for 70 years and then they would return. That means that the adults would not return to their land, but their children would, because the adults would have died by then.

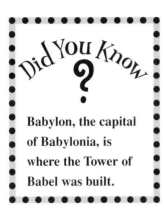

Did You Know?

Babylon, the capital of Babylonia, is where the Tower of Babel was built.

Babylonia was great for less than 100 years. Then the Medes and Persians conquered them, and the Persian Empire took over.

More is written about the people returning to their homeland in the books of Ezra and Nehemiah.

1 & 2 Chronicles

The author is not known but many people believe that Ezra wrote these books.

1 Chronicles repeats much of the Jewish history already given in 2 Samuel and 1 & 2 Kings. The first few chapters give us David's list of ancestors from Adam to Abraham to Jacob and through the many kings in David's family. Other lists of people are also given. The rest of the book talks about David's reign as king.

2 Chronicles retells Solomon becoming king and the building of the temple. It tells of the other kings who followed Solomon.

One of these kings was Josiah. Josiah became king when he was only eight years old. While the temple was being repaired, the workers found the Book of the Law. It has God's laws in it. When it was read to Josiah, he was very sad. He knew the people weren't following God. He destroyed all the idols and told the people to worship God.

Even though Josiah was a good king, the people often turned to idol worship, so God allowed them to be defeated. The temple at Jerusalem was destroyed and the city wall was broken down.

2 Chronicles ends 70 years later when the king of Persia gives the people permission to return to Jerusalem to rebuild the temple.

Ezra

Even though the book of Ezra doesn't say who wrote it, Ezra probably wrote this book along with the Chronicles. The book is named for the main character, a man who followed God.

☞ Do It

Do the crossword puzzle to learn more about the book of Ezra. All references are from the book of Ezra. The solution is on page 192.

Word List

altar	Babylon	cedar
Cyrus	Darius	Haggai
house	Jerusalem	Jeremiah
Lebanon	Nebuchadnezzar	Seraiah
seven	sins	Zechariah

Across

3. Place the temple would be built. (1:5)
7. King who took the Jews captive. (2:1)
9. King of Persia who let the Jews return to rebuild the temple. (1:1-4)
10. Ezra's father. (7:1)
12. Ezra confessed the people's _____. (9:5-6)
13. Prophet who told the people to continue rebuilding the temple after enemies made them afraid. (5:1)
14. Number of days the people celebrated the Feast of the Unleavened Bread. (6:22)

Down

1. The temple was the _____ of the Lord. (1:5)
2. A latter king of Persia. (4:5)
3. He prophesied the length of time the people would be captives. (1:1)
4. Where sacrifices were offered. (3:2)
5. Type of logs used. (3:7)
6. Capital of Babylonia where the people were held captive. (2:1)

8. Another prophet who told the people to continue the work on the temple. (5:1)

11. Where the logs for the temple were brought from. (3:7)

The Jews returned to their land in more than one group. A group of about 43,000 Jews returned to rebuild the temple in Jerusalem. After they laid the foundation, the idol worshippers who had lived there while the Jews were in captivity offered to help rebuild the temple. The Jews did not want idol worshippers to help build a temple meant for worshipping God. This made the idol worshippers so mad that they started spreading lies and rumors about God's people, which delayed the rebuilding of the temple for almost 18 years!

Then the prophets Haggai and Zechariah told the people to restart the work on the temple. The temple only took four years longer to finish, but that was 22 years total. The new temple wasn't nearly as grand as the one that Solomon had built.

Fifty-eight years after the temple was finished, Ezra arrived with a second group that included almost 2,000 men. He found that the people and even the priests had married wives who worshipped idols. Ezra told the people they were wrong. He confessed the sins to God and the people promised to obey God.

Nehemiah (Nehemiah was probably the author of this book but Ezra may have helped.)

The book of Ezra told about two groups of Jews who returned to their land. The book of Nehemiah tells about a third group who returned and rebuilt the city wall.

Nehemiah was a cupbearer to the Persian king Artaxerxes. It was a very important job and the king trusted Nehemiah. Nehemiah heard that the city walls were destroyed around Jerusalem. This meant that enemies could easily overrun Jerusalem. Nehemiah was very sad about this so the king allowed him to return home to rebuild the walls.

Nehemiah inspected the wall to see what needed to be done. Then he gave different groups of people sections of the wall to repair. Some enemies didn't want the wall rebuilt. They were afraid that the Jews would become powerful again. Nehemiah had an official letter from the king saying he was allowed to rebuild the walls so the enemies couldn't stop the work on the walls.

Nehemiah prayed for God's help in rebuilding the walls. He also put guards around the city to keep enemies from ruining their work. The wall was completed in only 52 days! Everyone knew that God had helped the people do this.

After the wall was rebuilt, Ezra read God's laws to the Israelites. They repented their sins and worshipped God. They agreed to obey God and not marry people who didn't worship God.

Esther (The author of Esther is unknown.)

In the book of Ezra, a first group of 43,000 left Persia to rebuild the temple. Later, Ezra led a group of 2,000 home. The book of Esther took place in Persia between the first and the second group leaving Persia.

King Ahasuerus (Xerxes) wanted his wife, Queen Vashti, to be part of a great celebration. The queen wouldn't do it, so she was sent away. Now the king needed a new queen. The king chose Esther, a young and beautiful Jew.

Esther's cousin Mordecai was a high official in the government. He told her not to tell the king that she was a Jew.

There was another official in the government who was more important than Mordecai. His name was Haman and he wanted everyone to bow when he came by. Mordecai wouldn't do it and Haman was furious. Haman learned that Mordecai was Jewish and he plotted to have all the Jewish people killed. He even built gallows to hang Mordecai!

One night when the king couldn't sleep, he asked that the book of records be read to him. The records said that Mordecai had once told the king of a plot against him. Mordecai had never been rewarded for it. The king ordered Haman to honor Mordecai for it. This was not part of Haman's plan!

Then Esther told the king that she was Jewish, and that Haman was going to have her people killed. Haman was hanged on the very gallows that he had built for Mordecai!

The king had already given the command to kill the Jews because of Haman, and the command couldn't be changed according to the laws. A new order was given that the Jews could get together and defend themselves. The Jews were able to save themselves. Mordecai became second in command to the king.

The people celebrated and had a feast that was called The Feast of Purim. It is still celebrated every year.

News Flash!

The book of Nehemiah (the events in Esther happened before Nehemiah) and the rebuilding of the wall bring us to the end of the Old Testament history. The books that come after Esther were written during the events described in the earlier books. The books of prophecy tell about prophets who gave the people God's messages during the events of 1 & 2 Kings, 1 & 2 Chronicles, Ezra and Nehemiah.

Chapter Four

Songs and Sayings

The Poetry Books aren't really books of poems. Job (that's JOBE, not a place to earn a paycheck!) is about a man who lost everything but still trusted God. Psalms is a book of songs that range from confessions to praises. Proverbs is a book of wisdom written by the wise King Solomon. Ecclesiastes was also written by Solomon, who tells what he learned about what is and isn't important in life.

Job

Kierra ran into homeroom just as the bell rang. Her shirt was dirty, and books and papers spilled out of her backpack.

"What happened to you?" Megan whispered.

"Everything!" Kierra said. "First my alarm didn't go off so I didn't get up in time to finish my math homework. Then my brother ate the last doughnut and I had to eat cereal. I hate cereal! I left my shoes outside yesterday and they were soaked this morning so I'm wearing yucky shoes. And to top it off, I fell off my bike right beside the bike rack! What else could go wrong?"

"Nothing, I hope. But at least things aren't as bad as they were for Job," Megan said.

"Who?" asked Kierra.

"Job. In the Old Testament. Now he was a man who had everything go wrong for him!"

The writer of Job is unknown. Job lived at the same time as Abraham, who we read about back in Genesis.

Job loved God. He had a family and owned a lot of things. Satan told God that Job only loved him because he had so much. Satan asked God if he could test Job. Some awful things happened to Job. You can read about it for yourself.

 Read It

Look up Job 1:1-3 and fill in the numbers below.

Job had:

_____ sons   _____ daughters

_____ sheep   _____ camels

_____ yoke of oxen   _____ donkeys

and a large number of servants!

What did God tell Satan he could do? (Job 1:12)

_____

Then awful things happened! What are some of the things that happened to Job? (Job 1:13-19)

_____

Everything Job had–except for himself and his wife–was gone. Satan still wasn't satisfied. What happened to Job next? (Job 2:4-8)

_____

Three friends came to Job and told him that all this must have happened because he was being punished for sin. What did Job tell them? (Job 27:5-6)

_____

Finally a fourth friend came and told Job that sometimes God has a reason for allowing bad things to happen to good people. It doesn't mean you are being punished for sin.

God spoke to the first three friends. What did He tell them? (Job 42:7-8)

_____

What did God do for Job? (Job 42:10-15)

Wow! A lot of bad things happened to Job, didn't they? Job must have wondered what was going on. All of these tragedies happened in the same day, and almost everything Job had was gone.

☞ Do It

What did Job say about losing everything? Use the phone below to help you decode Job's words. The first number tells you which button of the phone to use. The second number tells you which letter to use. Example, 3.2 means use the number three button. The .2 means to use the second letter on that button which is "e."

8.1 4.2 3.2   5.3 6.3 7.2 3.1   4.1 2.1 8.3 3.2   2.1 6.2 3.1   8.1 4.2 3.2

5.3 6.3 7.2 3.1   4.2 2.1 7.3   8.1 2.1 5.2 3.2 6.2   2.1 9.1 2.1 9.3;

_____ _____ _____ _____ _____

6.1 2.1 9.3   8.1 4.2 3.2   6.2 2.1 6.1 3.2   6.3 3.3   8.1 4.2 3.2

_____ _____ _____

5.3 6.3 7.2 3.1   2.2 3.2   7.1 7.2 2.1 4.3 7.3 3.2 3.1.

Answer: The Lord gave and the Lord has taken away; may the name of the Lord be praised. (Job 1:21)

Job still trusted in God. He didn't blame God for all the bad things that happened.

Satan wasn't satisfied. He went back to God and told Him that Job would curse Him if Job himself were harmed. God allowed Satan to harm Job, but told him that Job could not be killed (see Job 2:1-10).

Satan caused Job to be covered with painful sores from head to toe! Job sat down in ashes and used a piece of broken pot to scrape his skin. His wife came to him and said, "Are you still holding on to your pride? Curse God and die!"

Job answered, "You are talking like a foolish woman. Should we accept good from God, and not trouble?"

Job continued to do what was right. Three friends came to Job and told him that all of this must have happened because he was being punished for sin. They didn't believe Job when he said he hadn't done anything wrong.

Finally a fourth friend came and told Job that sometimes God has a reason for allowing bad things to happen to good people. It doesn't mean you are being punished for sin. God spoke to the first three friends and told them that they were wrong.

During all that happened, Job trusted God. God rewarded Job by giving him good health, new children and more animals and riches than he had ever had before.

Psalms

David wrote 73 of the
150 Psalms. Several people
wrote the others. The Psalms
are not all alike. There are
seven kinds of psalms.

 Praise psalms show
us how to praise God.
Read Psalm 33. Write your favorite verse from this psalm.

_____

_____

 History psalms remind us of what God did for His people. Read
Psalm 106:7-24. It tells of many of the events you've already
learned about in this book. Write the events that you remember
from earlier parts of the Bible.

_____

_____

3 Friendship psalms remind us that God loves us and that we
should show our love to Him. Read Psalm 23. What did David
say God did for him?

_____

4 Anger psalms ask God to punish evil people. Read Psalm 35.
The psalm asks for deliverance and help, but at the end the
writer praises God. Write his verse of praise and remember it
throughout the day.

_____

_____

5 Confession psalms ask forgiveness for sins. Read Psalm 51. What did David ask God to do in verse 7?

_____

6 Messiah psalms tell about Jesus. Read Psalm 22:1, 6-8, 12-13 and 28. What do they say about Jesus?

_____

_____

7 Worship psalms were used on special religious holidays. Read Psalm 30. This was a song for committing the completed temple to God. Find and write the verse that tells when joy will come.

_____

 # Memorize It

Shout for joy to the Lord, all the earth. Worship the Lord with gladness; come before him with joyful songs. Know that the Lord is God. It is he who made us, and we are his; we are his people, the sheep of his pasture. Enter his gates with thanksgiving and his courts with praise; give thanks to him and praise his name. For the Lord is good and his love endures forever; his faithfulness continues through all generations.

~Psalm 100:1-5

In Bible times, the Psalms were used for prayer and praise in the temple and synagogues. Do you ever sing praise songs at church that come from the Psalms? Listen to what you sing over the next few weeks and write down any songs that come from the Psalms.

_____

_____

Proverbs

Wise King Solomon wrote most of the book of Proverbs. 1 Kings 4:32 says that Solomon told 3,000 proverbs and wrote 1,005 songs. The proverbs are people's wisdom, not promises from God. They tell us how to make good decisions and do the right thing.

☞ Do It

Complete the following crossword puzzle by filling in the missing words from Proverbs. A reference is given for each proverb. The solution is on page 192.

Word List

actions	blameless	commands	crown
faithfulness	forsake	gentle	heart
honeycomb	listen	rubies	succeed
tongue	wealth	wisdom	

Across

2. A _____ answer turns away wrath (15:1).

4. Let love and _____ never leave you (3:3).

6. Let the wise _____ and add to their learning (1:5).

7. Pleasant words are a _____ sweet to the soul and healing the bones (16:24).

10. Honor the Lord with your _____ (3:9).

12. My son, keep your father's _____ (6:20).

13. A wife of noble character who can find? She is worth far more than _____ (31:10).

Down

1. Even a child is known by his _____, by whether his conduct is pure and right (20:11).

3. He who holds his _____ is wise (10:19).

4. Do not _____ your mother's teaching (1:8).

5. Commit to the Lord whatever you do, and your plans will _____ (16:3).

8. Better a poor man whose walk is _____ than a rich man whose ways are perverse (28:6).

9. The fear of the Lord is the beginning of _____ (9:10).

11. Above all else, guard your _____, for it is the wellspring of life (4:23).

12. A wife of noble character is her husband's _____ (12:4).

Ecclesiastes

Solomon wrote Ecclesiastes. He calls himself "teacher" in the book. He wrote this book near the end of his life after he had started worshipping idols.

Ecclesiastes shows us that even the richest and smartest people cannot be happy unless they know God.

The book of Ecclesiastes is Solomon's search for meaning in life. Ecclesiastes 1:2 says "'Meaningless, meaningless!' says the teacher. 'Utterly meaningless! Everything is meaningless.'" Solomon spends six chapters talking about everything that is meaningless to him. For the rest of the book he tells how to make the best of a meaningless life.

☞ Do It

In the final verses of Ecclesiastes, Solomon reaches the truth. What does he tell us is the "conclusion of the matter"? To find out, write the letter that comes between the two letters given.

_____ _____ _____ _____
EG DF ZB QS   FH NP CE   ZB MO CE   JL DF DF OQ

_____ _____
GI HJ RT   BD NP LN LN ZB MO CE LN DF MO SU RT,

_____ _____ _____ _____
EG NP QS   SU GI HJ RT   HJ RT   SU GI DF

_____ _____ _____ _____
VX GI NP KM DF   CE TV SU XZ   NP EG   LN ZB MO.

Answer: Fear God and keep his commandments, for this is the whole duty of man. (Ecclesiastes 12:13)

98

Song of Solomon

Solomon wrote Song of Solomon, sometimes called Song of Songs, when he was young, during the early years of his reign as king.

Song of Solomon is about a man and woman who are married. Most people believe that Solomon wrote this when he was married to just one woman. This woman was his true love. Later, Solomon married many more wives, as was the custom in Old Testament times.

This book doesn't mention God, but God uses it to show us that the love between a married man and woman is very beautiful and meaningful. Some of the writing in the book sounds sort of "mushy," as when Solomon tells his true love, "Your eyes are doves" (Song 1:15) and "Your hair is like a flock of goats descending from Mount Gilead" (Song 4:1). You probably wouldn't like it if someone told you that your hair was like a flock of goats! But at that time it was a compliment.

Once Solomon started marrying other women, he changed. Many of his wives worshipped idols and he began to worship idols with them. That's why it's important when you begin to date to ask God to help you make good choices about who you date and, later, who you marry. Make sure the guys you date love God and want to live the way God wants them to live. That's the only way to be happy. And that's one lesson wise King Solomon missed!

Chapter Five

Prophetic Announcements

Part One!

The titles "major prophets" and "minor prophets" are used because of the lengths of the books, not because some prophets were more important than others were. The books of the major prophets are much longer than those of the minor prophets.

The prophets were people called by God to take His messages to different countries and leaders. God sent prophets to visit nations that were sinning. Prophets told the people to repent and they told them what would happen if they didn't give up their sinful ways. Because of this, the prophets were not always liked. Sometimes they had to go to the king of a country and tell the king that he was sinning. This was not easy because they didn't know how the king would react.

Isaiah

Isaiah wrote the book that has his name.

Remember that the 12 tribes divided? The Northern Kingdom was Israel. It had 10 tribes. The Southern Kingdom was Judah. It had two tribes.

Isaiah was a prophet to the Southern Kingdom. He lived during the time that Assyria took captive the Northern Kingdom. Isaiah gave God's message to Judah. He told the people that Babylon would capture Judah. And later it happened!

Isaiah not only told the people how God would judge them, he also told them that a Savior was coming. Look up and read the verses at the top of the next page. Write what each one says about Jesus. Keep in mind that they were written long before Jesus was born!

Isaiah 7:14

_____

_____

Isaiah 53:5

_____

_____

☞ Do It

Isaiah heard God asking, "Whom shall I send? And who will go for us?" What did Isaiah say? Use the clocks below to help you find the solution. The answer is below.

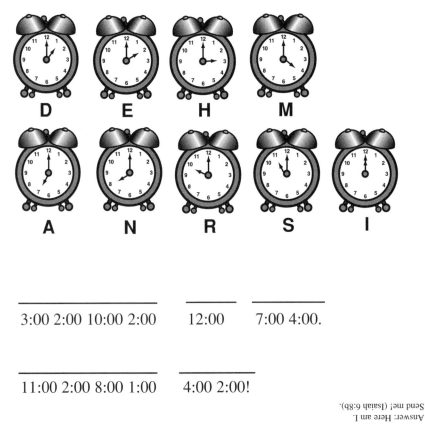

3:00 2:00 10:00 2:00   12:00   7:00 4:00.

11:00 2:00 8:00 1:00   4:00 2:00!

"**W**ay to go Eagles, way to go," Jessi chanted along with the cheerleaders who were on the sidelines of the basketball court.

Jessi's cousin Cassie was visiting her and had come to watch the game.

"Hey, that's funny," Cassie said. "Our team name is Eagles, too."

Jessi and Cassie jumped up and cheered as Jessi's brother Mike scored the first basket. An exciting game followed with the Eagles leading all the way. At the final buzzer, the score was 84-60.

"Yes," screamed Jessi. "Way to go Eagles!"

Have you noticed that there are a lot of teams named Eagles but none named Sparrows or Hummingbirds or Robins? That's because eagles are thought of as mighty birds. Not all eagles are large, though. One of the smallest is the Little eagle of Australia. From wing tip to wing tip, it is only about three feet wide. On the other hand, the female Bald eagle can have wings that are almost eight feet long.

An eagle's body is made for flying and catching prey. The body is lightweight and very strong. One reason it is lightweight is that the eagle's bones are hollow. The skeleton of a Bald eagle only weighs a little more than half a pound. And the Bald eagle's 7,000 feathers only weigh about 21 ounces all together.

As an eagle flaps its mighty wings, air flows faster over the top of the wings, and the eagle rises into the sky. The eagle can float thousands of feet above us without flapping its wings at all.

Did you know that the book of Isaiah talks about eagles? Isaiah 40:31 says, "But those who hope in the Lord will renew their strength. They will soar on wings like eagles; they will run and not grow weary, they will walk and not faint."

What a great promise! When we trust in God, He gives us strength just as He gives the eagle that soars in the sky. Think about Isaiah 40:31 when you are tired or discouraged. Trust God and soar like an eagle!

Memorize It

But those who hope in the Lord will renew their strength. They will soar on wings like eagles; they will run and not grow weary, they will walk and not faint.

~Isaiah 40:31

Jeremiah

Jeremiah wrote the book that has his name. He was also a prophet to Judah, the Southern Kingdom. Jeremiah started giving the people God's messages during the reign of Josiah, the boy who became king at age eight.

Jeremiah spoke to the people of Judah during the times that they sinned the most. The people worshipped idols. God promised to punish them. He said they would be captured and taken to Babylon. Jeremiah was rejected and even thrown in prison for telling the people God's message.

The end of Jeremiah tells how the city of Jerusalem was destroyed and how the people were taken captive. The city of Jerusalem was burned, including the beautiful temple King Solomon had built.

Jeremiah is called "the weeping prophet." He was sad because of the punishments that the people received. He knew God was fair, but it was hard to see Judah punished. People made fun of Jeremiah. He must have felt alone and rejected, but he shared his feelings with God (see Jeremiah 15:15, 17-18).

Are there times you feel lonely or like you are the only one who is doing what is right? Write a prayer to God, telling Him how you feel.

_____

_____

 # Memorize It

(This was written to the people while they were captives but it is still true today.)

"For I know the plans I have for you," declares the Lord, "plans to prosper you and not to harm you, plans to give you hope and a future."

~Jeremiah 29:11

Lamentations

Jeremiah wrote this sad book of the Bible. "Lamentations" means "to cry out loud." Jeremiah was very unhappy about the destruction of Jerusalem and the temple. For 40 years, Jeremiah warned the people to turn from their sins. They wouldn't listen and God punished them just as He said He would.

Have you ever sung the hymn "Great is thy Faithfulness"? It is based on Lamentations 3:22-23: "Because of the Lord's great love we are not consumed, for his compassions never fail. They are new every morning; great is your faithfulness."

Ezekiel

Ezekiel wrote the book with his name. He was a prophet to the Jews while they were captives in Babylon. He told them that they were captives because of their sins. Before they could return to their land, he told them they must start obeying God.

Not all the people of Judah were taken to Babylon at the same time. Jeremiah was still in Jerusalem warning the people while Ezekiel was one of the captives taken to Babylon. God used visions to show Ezekiel what to tell the people.

One of the visions Ezekiel saw was of dry bones scattered in a valley (see Ezekiel 37:1-14). The bones went back together and were covered with flesh but weren't alive until the breath of life was given to them. God told him that the bones stood for the Jewish people scattered

throughout the nations. The bones coming back together stood for the people being gathered again in the Promised Land. God's spirit would give them life.

Daniel

Daniel wrote the book that has his name. You have probably heard a lot of stories about Daniel at church.

Three different groups of captives were

taken from Judah to Babylon. When Nebuchadnezzar conquered Jerusalem, he asked for the best young men to be taken to Babylon in the first group. Daniel and his three friends were in this first group. They were only young men at the time.

The young men were trained to serve in the king's palace. They were given the best food, but Daniel and his friends wouldn't eat it (see Daniel 1:8-15). Why not? God had rules about how the Jews should prepare their food. This food wasn't prepared according to God's laws, and some of it had been offered to idols.

Do It

What did Daniel and his friends want to eat instead of the king's food? Start with the first letter and write every other letter on the line to find out.

VHETGOENTEALBELEOEPS BATNED WWIALTOEAR

Answer: vegetables and water (Daniel 1:12)

Days later, when it was time to go before the king, Daniel and his friends were healthier and smarter than any of the other young men who had eaten the king's rich food.

QUIZ! Answer It

Are You a Daniel?

When Daniel was taken captive to Babylon, he was asked to eat food that he knew he shouldn't eat. He decided that he would do the right thing and not eat the food. There were many other times that Daniel did the right thing even if he had to do it alone. Are you like Daniel? Take this quiz and find out.

1 The teacher in the room next to your classroom asks your teacher to come over for just a minute. Your teacher tells you to read your library books quietly for a few minutes while she's gone. As soon as she leaves, everyone starts talking to each other. You:

a. Whisper to your neighbor. After all, whispering isn't really talking!

b. Read your library book quietly. You can probably read at least two pages while your teacher is gone.

c. Talk with the others. You won't be the only one to be in trouble if you get caught.

2 You are in a hurry to put your backpack in your bedroom so you can go over to your neighbor Justine's house. As you run through the living room, you bump into a vase and knock it over. It breaks. No one but the cat is anywhere around. You:

a. Get rid of the pieces. Maybe nobody will notice it's missing.

b. Clean it up. Tell your mom what happened and offer to save your allowance to replace it.

c. Leave the vase. Run over to Justine's before anyone knows you're home and hope your mom thinks the cat broke the vase.

3 You really want to get your Bible club memory award but you are stuck on one verse. Then you realize that your leader accidentally signed that one off last week. You:

a. Decide not to tell her since you almost have the verse learned. You plan to go back and finish it later anyway.

b. Tell the leader about the mistake. Ask her to help you learn the verse.

c. Ignore it. It was her mistake, not yours!

4 You can't remember how to spell "indivisible" during your spelling test. Just as the teacher calls "time's up," you accidentally see the word on your friend's test. You:

a. Copy it down. You knew how to spell it but just forgot for a second.

b. Turn your test paper in without it. Start studying ahead for next week's spelling test.

c. Copy it down. You didn't mean to see her paper so it wasn't like you cheated!

5 Brittany, the most popular girl in class, takes some candy out of the teacher's drawer. Then she tells the teacher that she saw Nathan, the class troublemaker, take it. Nathan gets sent to the office. You:

a. Ignore the situation. It doesn't concern you.

b. Talk to the teacher but wait until you can do it in private.

c. Nod your head in agreement with Brittany like the rest of the class is doing. No one wants to get in bad with Brittany.

How did you do? Count up all your a's, b's and c's.

Mostly a's: You try not to do the wrong thing, but you don't do the right thing either. Put your all into honesty and make the best choices. Do the right thing whether or not anyone will ever know. You know and God knows!

Mostly b's: You are a young Daniel. You do the right thing even if no one will know the difference and even when it's hard. Like Daniel, you stand up for God even if you have to do it alone. God will reward you for it.

Mostly c's: You need to think more carefully about your choices. Learn to always do right and you will stay out of trouble now and later in life.

One time while Daniel was away, the king built a golden statue of himself. He said everyone must bow down to it. Did the three friends bow to the statue? Read it for yourself.

 Read It

Read Daniel 3 and then answer the questions below.

How big was the statue that Nebuchadnezzar made? (verse 1)

_____

How did the people know when it was time to bow to the statue? (verse 7)

_____

Who did not worship the statue? (verse 12)

_____

What would happen to them? (verse 11)

_____

What did the king see? (verse 25)

_____

Where the three men harmed? (verse 27)

_____

What new order did Nebuchadnezzar give? (verse 29)

_____

Do you think it was easy or hard for the three men to refuse to bow to the statue? Why?

_____

When is it hardest for you to stand up for what you believe?

_____

Daniel became important to Nebuchadnezzar because God helped Daniel tell Nebuchadnezzar what some of his dreams meant. After Nebuchadnezzar died, Darius became king and appointed Daniel as one of the three rulers over the kingdom. Daniel did a good job, so King Darius wanted to make him even more important. But the other two rulers were jealous and came up with a plan to get rid of Daniel. Read about it below (also see Daniel 6:5-23).

 Read It

Daniel

King Darius

bad men

pray(ed)

lions

 was a hard worker. became very important in

's kingdom. Some were jealous. They wanted to get in trouble. The knew that to his God three times a day. The tricked into making a law that said all people must only to . still to God. The arrested him and threw him into a den of . God protected . The next morning went to see what happened to . called, " , was your God able to protect you?" answered, "God sent his angel, and he shut the mouths of the ." was taken from the pit of and the were thrown to the instead. made a new law that everyone must worship the true God.

The rest of the book of Daniel tells about visions he saw. Many of the events he told about happened later in his own lifetime. More happened after he died, and some will happen in the future.

All of these prophets kept their ears open to hear what God would tell them, and their hearts open to obey what He told them to do. You can hear God's message today by listening in church and reading the Bible for yourself. You can obey Him by doing the things the Bible says God wants you to do.

Chapter Six

Prophetic Announcements

Part Two!

There are 12 books that are called "Minor Prophets." Remember that they are only called Minor Prophets because the books are shorter than the Major Prophets, not because they are less important.

Each prophet took God's message to a certain group of people. Some prophesied to the Northern Kingdom and some to the Southern Kingdom. Some of the prophets spoke to the Jews who returned to Jerusalem from being captives (in exile). Others talked to those in Nineveh, Babylon and Edom.

Each book is named for the person who wrote it.

Hosea

Hosea gave God's message to Israel, the Northern Kingdom.

Hosea's name means "savior." In a way, he was a savior. God asked Hosea to do a hard thing: He asked him to marry a woman who wouldn't be faithful to him. Every time Hosea's wife went to other men, Hosea went after her and brought her home. This was a picture of how God brought His own people back each time they sinned and turned away from Him. Hosea warned the people to turn back to God. But they didn't, and the Northern Kingdom was taken captive.

Joel

Joel spoke to Judah, the Southern Kingdom.

Joel begins with a description of a plague of locusts that covered the land and ruined the crops.

People still have problems with grasshoppers today. The state of Utah recently had trouble with grasshoppers. One lady called the grasshoppers "crunchy bags of goo." Imagine how it would be to live in a whole land covered with locusts!

Joel told the people that the locusts were God's punishment for their sins. He said the land would be taken over by an enemy if they didn't repent.

Amos

Amos prophesied to Israel.

Amos lived six miles south of Bethlehem in a village in the Judean hills. He was a sheep farmer who also grew sycamore trees. He told the people that God would punish them for their sins. The people didn't like the shepherd from the hills. He preached against them for worshipping idols and treating the poor people unkindly.

Amos told the people about five visions God had shown him. These visions all meant that God was going to punish the people of Israel for their bad behavior.

Amos asked God several times to spare the people, and He did. But finally, God said He would not spare them any longer. However, God did promise that after the people learned their lessons by being taken captive, He would return them to their land.

Obadiah

Obadiah spoke to those in Edom. Edom is near Judah.

One of God's promises to Abraham was, "I will bless those who bless you, and whoever curses you I will curse" (Genesis 12:3). The Edomites attacked Judah and looted Jerusalem at least four times. Obadiah told the people that God would destroy Edom for what it had done to Judah.

The people of Edom were happy when Babylon captured Judah. Obadiah told the people that someday God would return His people to their land and also give them Edom.

Jonah

Jonah went to Nineveh–reluctantly at first (see Jonah 1:1–2:10).

 Do It

Do this crossword puzzle to test your knowledge of Jonah. All references are from the book of Jonah. The solution is on page 192.

Word List

afraid   Amittai   angry   cargo   captain
destruction fish   forty   Hebrew   Nineveh
prayed   sea   shade   storm   Tarshish   worm

Across

2. The sailors threw this into the sea to lighten the ship (1:5).
3. Where Jonah told the sailors to throw him (1:12).
4. Jonah did this for three days and nights (2:1).
9. Jonah's dad (1:1).
10. Jonah felt this way when God spared the people because they repented (4:1).
12. Jonah tried to run away to this place (1:3).
14. This chewed through a vine (4:7).
15. Jonah told the people that they would be destroyed in this many days (3:4).

Down

1. This swallowed Jonah (1:17).
2. He woke up Jonah on the ship (1:6).
5. When the people repented, God did not bring this (3:10).
6. God told Jonah to go here (1:2).
7. God sent this to punish Jonah (1:4).
8. God provided this for Jonah (4:5).
11. How the sailors felt (1:5).
13. Jonah said he was of these people (1:9).

Micah

Micah prophesied in Judah.

Micah was a prophet before either the Northern or Southern Kingdoms were taken captive. Micah spoke to the people about false prophets, dishonest leaders and ungodly priests. He told these wicked people that they would be punished. He urged them to confess their sins and turn back to God.

Micah pictured God as a judge in a courtroom accusing His people. Micah said, "The Lord has a case against His people."

Micah also prophesied that Israel would have a great king, born in Bethlehem, who would bring strength and peace (see Micah 5:2).

Who was that king? _____

✝ Memorize It

And what does the Lord require of you? To act justly and to love mercy and to walk humbly with your God.

~Micah 6:8

Nahum

Nahum spoke to the people in Nineveh. Nineveh was the capital of Assyria. Assyria had captured the Northern Kingdom.

Nahum was written about 150 years after Jonah went to Nineveh. When Jonah gave God's message to the people, they stopped sinning and they turned back to God. Now they were wicked and cruel again.

Nahum described how Nineveh would be captured by the Babylonians. He said that a great flood would destroy the city walls, and Nineveh would be burned. Nineveh had great wealth and strength and massive walls. They didn't think anything could destroy them, but it all happened just as Nahum had said it would.

Habakkuk

Habakkuk was a prophet to Judah after the Northern Kingdom had been captured by Assyria and Assyria captured by Babylon. The Southern Kingdom had not yet been conquered by the Babylonians.

The book of Habakkuk is a conversation between Habakkuk and God. It is full of questions and answers.

Habakkuk asks God something like, "Why aren't the people of Judah being punished for the wicked things they are doing?" (see Habakkuk 1:1-11)

God answers, "The Babylonians will punish Judah."

Habakkuk asks, "Why use a wicked nation like Babylon? Babylon is worse than Judah!"

God answers "Babylon will be punished in My time."

After Habakkuk understood what God was going to do, Habakkuk praised God for His power and holiness.

Zephaniah

Zephaniah was a prophet to Judah during Josiah's reign. Some of the people had become very rich by being unfair to the poor. These people also worshipped idols. Zephaniah encouraged Josiah to do what was right.

King Josiah listened to Zephaniah and tried to get the people to worship God. He tore down the idols and the altars used to worship the idols. He read part of God's law to the people. Even though Josiah attempted to turn the people back to God, it was too late. Josiah was Judah's last godly king.

Like many of the other prophets, Zephaniah warned the people of God's judgment. He also gave them hope that one day God would bring His people back to their land.

Haggai

Haggai prophesied to the Jews, who had returned to Jerusalem. The Jews started to rebuild the temple but then had to stop to clear the land, plant crops and build homes. (Judah had been ruined when the Jews were taken captive.) Because of all this extra work, the Jews became discouraged. Haggai encouraged them to finish the temple. The people listened to Haggai and started rebuilding the temple again.

 Make It

Bible Promise Box

God spoke to the prophets about things that were going to happen. Sometimes He warned them of bad things to come. Other times He gave them promises such as:

Therefore tell the people: This is what the Lord Almighty says: "Return to me," declares the Lord Almighty, "and I will return to you," says the Lord Almighty.

~ Zechariah 1:3

When you read your Bible, look for promises from God. You can put them in your **Bible Promise Box**.

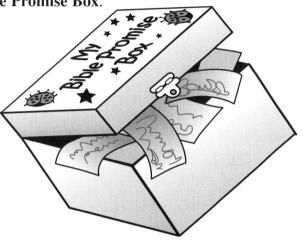

What You Need

* unpainted wooden box
* paint
* stickers for designs
* marker or paint
* small strips of paper
* pen or pencil

What to Do

1. You can get small, unpainted wooden boxes for about a dollar at a craft store.
2. Use your favorite color of paint to paint the outside of the box. Allow it to dry and give it a second coat if needed.
3. Write "My Bible Promise Box" on the lid with a marker or paint.
4. Decorate the box with stickers.
5. Whenever you read a verse that has a promise from God, write it on a strip of paper and put it in the box. (Matthew 7:7 and Hebrews 13:5 are good promise verses to start with).
6. Read the verses from your Bible Promise Box when you are feeling discouraged.

Zechariah

Zechariah also prophesied to the Jews who had returned to Jerusalem. Along with Haggai, he encouraged the Jews to rebuild the temple. One night, God gave Zechariah eight visions about restoring Jerusalem and about the good future the Jews would have. Zechariah told them Christ would come as both a man and a judge of the nations to rule the world.

Malachi

Malachi prophesied to all the Jews who returned to Jerusalem after they were captives. The people fell into sin again. They worshipped idols, and they married people who worshipped idols. Malachi ends the Old Testament by reminding the people that God loves them and wants to bless them if they follow Him.

 Make It

Tithe and Offering Bank

The Bible tells us that we should give part of our money to God (see Malachi 3:8-10). This is called "tithing," which means giving 10 percent of our money to God's work. Money that is more than our tithe, or ten percent, is our offering. Even though you probably don't have a regular job like your mom or dad, you might receive an allowance or gift money. Make this church-shaped tithe and offering bank to help you remember to set aside money for God's work.

What You Need

* small milk carton (like in your school lunch)
* scissors or knife
* white paint
* paint for roof
* cellophane
* stapler
* tape

What to Do

1. Thoroughly rinse and clean the carton.

2. Open the carton and cut the corners down to the fold.

3. On the creased sides, trim off the corners so a triangle shape remains.

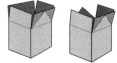

4. Have a parent help you cut window shapes on each side and in the front if desired. Cut a slit in the top for money.

5. Cut a small piece of cellophane and tape it over the window from the inside to make it look like a stained glass window from the outside. Do this for each window.

6. Have a parent help you cut a door in the front that you can open to get your money out of your bank.

7. Fold the top flaps to form a roof, and staple.

8. Paint the roof your choice of colors and allow to dry. (If the paint won't stick to the waxy surface, add a couple of drops of dish soap to it.)

9. Paint the church white and allow to dry.

10. Add other details or decorations.

11. Drop your tithe and offering money into your bank during the week. On Sunday, empty the bank and take the money to church for the offering plate.

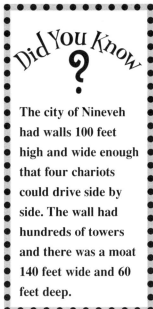

Did You Know?

The city of Nineveh had walls 100 feet high and wide enough that four chariots could drive side by side. The wall had hundreds of towers and there was a moat 140 feet wide and 60 feet deep.

✝ Between the Old and ✝ New Testaments

Here is a comparison of how things were when the Old Testament ends and the New Testament begins.

When the Old Testament ends...

✵ The Persians are in charge.

✵ There is a small temple in Jerusalem.

✵ There is no king over Judah.

✵ The people speak Hebrew.

When the New Testament begins...

✵ The Romans are in charge.

✵ There is a beautiful temple in Jerusalem.

✵ King Herod rules over Judah, now called Judea.

✵ Most people speak Greek.

✵ The land is divided into Galilee in the north, Judea in the south and Samaria in between.

Many changes took place in the 400 years between the Old Testament and the New Testament. After King Cyrus of Persia let the Jews go home, Persia ruled for another hundred years. Then Alexander the Great, from near Greece, took over. He decided the people should speak Greek. He wanted them to follow Greek ways of doing things, not Jewish ways.

About another hundred years later, the Syrians (not the Assyrians) took over. A big statue of the god Zeus was placed in the temple at Jerusalem. A pig was sacrificed on the altar to Zeus. This was wrong. God said pigs should never be sacrificed. They were not one of the animals God chose as sacrifices.

The Jews were very upset. Five brothers, the Maccabees, decided to fight Antiochus, who had done these evil things. The brothers captured Jerusalem and got rid of the statue. They rebuilt the altar of the Lord. The people were free again! A priest, not a king, now ruled them.

But then two of the brothers each decided that he wanted to be the high priest. They both asked Rome for help. Rome was the largest empire of all! The Romans didn't help in the way that either brother wanted. Instead, they took over the Jews' land (now called Palestine) and made it part of the Roman Empire.

Now the Romans were in charge. They allowed Herod to be king as long as he did what they told him to do. King Herod the Great built himself palaces. He hollowed out the top of a mountain to make a fortress. He built a new city and called it "Caesarea." He built the Jews a new, large temple to try to get them to like him. (The temple wasn't actually finished until long after his death.)

So when Jesus was born in Bethlehem, about five miles south of Jerusalem, Palestine was a small part of the great Roman Empire. But it was very important because it connected three continents: Europe, Asia, and Africa. The birth of Christ begins the New Testament.

Chapter Seven

Gospel Gems

You've already read what happened during Old Testament times. All of that set the stage for Jesus to be born. Jesus' birth, ministry, death and resurrection are what the New Testament is all about.

There are 27 books in the New Testament. Here is how they are grouped.

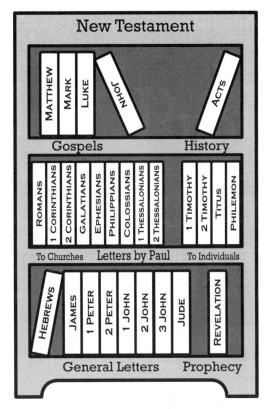

Gospels	Epistles	
Matthew	Romans	Philemon
Mark	1 & 2 Corinthians	Hebrews
Luke	Galatians	James
John	Ephesians	1 & 2 Peter
	Philippians	1, 2 & 3 John
History	Colossians	Jude
Acts	1 & 2 Thessalonians	
	1 & 2 Timothy	**Prophecy**
	Titus	Revelation

☜ Do It

Listed below are some of the books of the New Testament. Try to arrange them so that they all fit in the grid. Start with the longest ones first. Some letters are given to help you. The solution is on page 192.

Word List

Acts	Colossians	Corinthians	Ephesians	Galatians
Hebrews	James	John	Jude	Luke
Mark	Matthew	Philippians	Philemon	Romans
Thessalonians	Timothy	Titus		

The Gospels

The word "gospel" means "good news." The first three gospels–Matthew, Mark and Luke–are somewhat alike. They describe Jesus' birth, miracles, parables (stories with a lesson) and sermons. The fourth gospel, John, tells about those same things, but John writes more about Jesus' conversations and prayers than the other gospels do.

Jesus' life and work were spent mainly in two places: Galilee and Judea. The first three gospels take place mostly in Galilee. John writes mainly about what happened in Judea.

Who Jesus Is

Jenny sat in a chair in the corner, listening to people talk. It was her mother's birthday, and her mom's friends had planned a surprise party for her. now the house was full of different people who knew Jenny's mom.

"Karen was the best school teacher my children had when they were growing up," Jenny heard one lady tell another.

"She was a good school teacher, but she's one of our most dedicated Sunday school teachers, too. She has a way of getting the children to sit still and really listen to the Bible," Jenny heard the other lady respond.

"Well, since she's my daughter I guess I can brag about her, too," Jenny's grandmother told them. "She was a good daughter growing up. never caused us any trouble. Always did her homework without being told. I bet you have some good things to say about your mother, too, don't you, Jenny?"

"Sure, she's the best," Jenny said. And she meant it!

The two ladies, the grandmother and Jenny were all talking about the same person. One lady knew her as a schoolteacher, another knew her as a Sunday school teacher, the grandmother knew her as a daughter and Jenny knew her as a mother.

The Gospels talk about Jesus in the same way.

✳ Matthew describes Jesus as a king.

✳ Mark describes Jesus as a servant.

✳ Luke describes Jesus as the Son of Man.

✳ John describes Jesus as the Son of God.

All of them are right. Because they picture Jesus a different way, the writers all tell about Jesus in a different way in their books.

The gospels also were written for different groups of people.

✳ Matthew was written for the Jews. It shows that Jesus is the messiah for whom they were looking.

✳ Mark is for anyone who doesn't know about Jesus. It is faster to read because it's full of action words.

✳ Luke was written for people who are not Jews. It tells that Jesus cares about the poor and the "nobodies" of the world.

✳ John was written in simple language for anyone to read and understand.

Each gospel is named for the person who wrote it. We'll look at Jesus' life from all the gospels together rather than each gospel separately since so many of the stories about Jesus are the same in each gospel.

A Special Baby (Luke 1:5-25, 57)

Zechariah was a priest. One day when he was alone in the temple, an angel named Gabriel came to him and told him that his wife,

Elizabeth, would have a son. The angel said Zechariah should name his son "John." Zechariah was surprised. He and his wife were old! They had never been able to have children! Zechariah doubted the angel.

 Do It

What did the angel tell Zechariah would happen because Zechariah didn't believe the message? Use this radio code to help you find the answer. Each radio station in the code stands for a letter. For example FM 88 =A. For every radio station, look on the next page for the matching letter.

	A	B	C	D	E	H	I	J	K
FM	88	92	94	96	98	100	102	104	106

	L	N	O	P	R	S	T	U	W
AM	900	950	1000	1050	1100	1150	1200	1250	1300

_____   _____
FM100 FM98   FM94 AM1000 AM1250 AM900 FM96 AM950 AM1200

_____
AM1150 AM1050 FM98 FM88 FM106

_____   _____
AM1250 AM950 AM1200 FM102 AM900   FM104 AM1000 FM100 AM950

_____   _____
AM1300 FM88 AM1150   FM92 AM1000 AM1100 AM950.

Answer: He couldn't speak until John was born. (see Luke 1:20)

Jesus Is Born (Luke 1:26-38)

The same angel who talked to Zechariah appeared to Mary. He told her she was going to have a baby. She asked how she could have a baby when she wasn't even married. The angel told her it would be a miracle! The baby would be the Son of God.

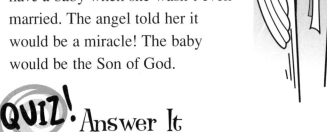

Answer It

How much do you know about Jesus' birth? Take the quiz below to find out.

1 Jesus' earthly father was:

    a. John   b. Zechariah   c. Joseph

2 This angel told Mary that she would give birth to Jesus.

    a. Michael   b. Gabriel   c. John

3 Mary visited this relative, who was also going to have a baby.

    a. Sarah   b. Elizabeth   c. Esther

4 This person said that everyone had to go back to the place where they were born to be counted.

    a. Caesar Augustus b. Herod   c. Zechariah

5 This is the town where Mary and Joseph went.

    a. Rome   b. Galilee   c. Bethlehem

6 Mary gave birth to Jesus and placed Him in this.

    a. manger   b. crib   c. baby swing

7 The angel of the Lord appeared to these people to tell them about Jesus' birth.

    a. kings   b. shepherds   c. priests

8 The angels said:

a. "Glory to God in the highest."   b. "Hallelujah."
c. "Praise the baby Jesus."

9 What led the Magi to Jesus?

a. map   b. star   c. camels

10 This king wanted to kill Jesus.

a. Nebuchadnezzar   b. Cyrus   c. Herod

Answers

1. **c.** Joseph. God was Jesus' real father, but Joseph was Mary's husband so he became Jesus' father while He lived on earth.
2. **b.** Gabriel brought messages to both Elizabeth and Mary.
3. **b.** Elizabeth. Both of these babies would be very important. John would tell others that someone great was coming who could forgive their sins. Jesus would be the Savior of the world.
4. **a.** Caesar Augustus. He said there must be a census. A census is when all the people are counted. Everyone had to go the town where he or she was born.
5. **c.** Bethlehem. Micah prophesied (in the Old Testament) that this is where Jesus would be born.
6. **a.** Manger. Because so many people were in the town to be counted, all the inns were full. Mary gave birth to Jesus in the stable.
7. **b.** Shepherds. They were in the fields with their sheep. How surprised they must have been to see an angel appear!
8. **a.** The angels said, "Glory to God in the highest, and on earth peace to men on whom his favor rests."
9. **b.** The Magi saw a special star in the east and followed it to Jesus.
10. **c.** Herod. You can read about him on page 123.

10 correct   Super! Give yourself a pat on the back!

7 or more correct   Good.

4-6 correct   Fair. Brush up on your facts about the most important birth of all times.

under 4 correct   Stop and read Luke chapter 2 and Matthew chapter 1, then try again.

Make It

Christmas Star Frame

Here is a fun star frame for you to make as a reminder of Jesus' birth. Hang it on your Christmas tree!

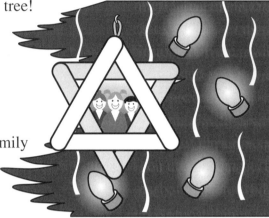

What You Need

* 6 craft sticks
* gold paint
* glue
* picture of yourself or family
* gold cord or wire

What to Do

1. Glue three craft sticks together to form a triangle.

2. Glue the second set of three craft sticks together to form a triangle.

3. Allow the glue to dry.

4. Place one triangle on top of the other to form a star. Glue.

5. Allow the glue to dry thoroughly.

6. Paint the frame gold (or another Christmas color). Add decorations if you like.

7. Cut the picture so the face shows through the opening but no part of the picture sticks out around the frame.

8. Glue the picture behind the frame.

9. Form a loop of cord and glue it to the top back of the frame for hanging. Allow to dry completely.

10. Hang on your tree!

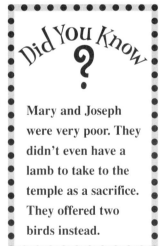

Did You Know?

Mary and Joseph were very poor. They didn't even have a lamb to take to the temple as a sacrifice. They offered two birds instead.

Three Groups to Remember

The Pharisees The Pharisees were men who claimed to follow every detail of God's law. They believed that both the Scriptures and the rabbis' (teachers of Old Testament law) teachings were equal. Jesus said this was wrong. He said the Scriptures were always correct, but what the rabbis said was sometimes wrong. So the Pharisees disliked Jesus.

The Sadducees These were wealthy men who controlled the priesthood. They believed only the first five books of the Old Testament were true Scripture. The Sadducees disagreed with the Pharisees about most things but they agreed with them in their hatred of Jesus. They saw Him as a threat to their power.

The Sanhedrin This was the highest Jewish court in Jesus' day.

Jesus' Childhood (Luke 2:41-52)

The Bible doesn't tell us much about Jesus' childhood. There is only one story in the Bible about Jesus when He was young. It is the story of when Jesus went to the temple when He was 12 years old. You can read it for yourself.

 Read It

Read Luke 2:39-52. Then answer the questions below.

What feast did Jesus and His parents go to every year? (verse 41)

Where did they live? (verse 39)

_____

Where was the feast (verse 41)?

_____

Was Jesus with His parents when they left to return home? (verse 43)

_____

Where did they think He was? (verse 44)

_____

How long was it before they found Him? Where was He? (verse 46)

_____

What was He doing? (verse 46)

_____

Jesus was talking about God with the teachers in the temple court. The teachers were amazed at how well Jesus understood about God. But they shouldn't have been, because Jesus was the Son of God!

Do you ever talk about God with church leaders? Do you ask questions in Sunday school to learn more about the lesson? This week, listen closely to your Sunday school lesson or the church sermon. Think of three questions to ask your teacher or pastor.

John the Baptist (Luke 3:1-22)

When John was an adult, he began preparing people for Jesus. John ate wild honey and grasshoppers. He wore a camel's hair coat. John preached near the Jordan River, east of Jerusalem.

Many people came to hear John. They believed what he said. But the Pharisees didn't!

Remember what happened between the Old and New Testaments?

Alexander the Great took over. He wanted everyone to act like Greeks. The Pharisees, who were Jews, wouldn't do it because they knew God had special laws for the Jews. John told the Pharisees that being a Jew wasn't enough. He said they had to repent and believe in Jesus. The Pharisees did not want to hear that!

Memorize It

For God so loved the world that he gave his one and only Son, that whoever believes in him shall not perish but have eternal life.
~John 3:16

John baptized people to show that they repented of their sins. One day, Jesus came to John to be baptized. John knew Jesus didn't need to repent of His sin because Jesus was perfect. Jesus wanted John to baptize Him, though, so John did. When Jesus was baptized, heaven opened and the Holy Spirit came from the sky in the form of a dove. Then a voice from heaven spoke.

Do It

What did the voice from heaven say? First, solve the problems below to make a key. Then use the key to decode the verse on the next page.

A= ____ 7+4   D= ____ 9-3   E= ____ 4+4   H= ____ 8-6

I= ____ 10+3   L= ____ 10-5   M= ____ 7-4   N= ____ 11-2

O= ____ 12-8   P= ____ 10-9   S= ____ 3+4   T= ____ 5+5

V= ____ 14+2   W= ____ 7+7   Y= ____ 10+5

10 2 13 7	13 7	3 15	7 4 9,	14 2 4 3	13

5 4 16 8;	14 13 10 2	2 13 3	13	11 3	14 8 5 5

1 5 8 11 7 8 6.

Answer: This is my Son, whom I love; with him I am well pleased. (Matthew 3:17)

After Jesus' baptism, He went into the desert, where Satan tempted Him. Every time Satan told Him to do something, Jesus answered by quoting Scripture. Finally, Jesus told Satan to get away from Him, and he did. When this test was over, Jesus started His ministry.

Jesus preached to people about the right ways to know God and love each other. He also chose 12 men to be His special followers, called "disciples." Here's a quick look at each disciple.

Name: Peter (also called "Simon" and "Simon Peter")
Brother of: Andrew, also a disciple
Job: fisherman
Special quality: Often said what was on his mind without thinking. (Sometimes he acted without thinking, too!)
Known for: Became a great preacher. Wrote the New Testament books 1 & 2 Peter.

Name: Andrew
Brother of: Peter, also a disciple
Job: fisherman
Special quality: Much quieter than his brother. Often brought people to Jesus one-by-one.
Known for: Heard about Jesus and believed in Him, then brought Peter to Jesus. Also brought the little boy with the loaves and fishes to Jesus.

Name: Matthew (also called Levi)
Job: tax collector
Special quality: Left dishonest job to follow Jesus.
Known for: Wrote the first gospel.

Name: Simon (also called "Simon the zealot")
Special quality: Was a zealot (a person who wanted to turn others against the Romans) before he met Jesus and changed his life.

Name: John
Brother of: James, also a disciple
Job: fisherman
Special quality: Was Jesus' closest friend.
Known for: Wrote the gospels of John; 1, 2, & 3 John and Revelation.

Name: Philip
From: the same town as Peter and Andrew (they may have been friends)
Job: fisherman
Special quality: Told others about Jesus.
Known for: Told Nathanael (Bartholomew) about Jesus. Also helped some Greek travelers meet Jesus.

Name: Thomas (also called "Didymus")
Known for: Became known as "Doubting Thomas" for doubting Jesus' resurrection, until he saw Him for himself!

Name: Thaddaeus (also known as "Judas, the son of James")
Known for: We do not know anything further about Thaddaeus. The Bible only gives us his name.

Name: James
Brother of: John, also a disciple
Job: fisherman
Special quality: His hot temper! Jesus called James and John the "sons of thunder"! (Once they wanted to call down fire on some villagers who wouldn't let them stay overnight!)

Name: Bartholomew (also called "Nathanael")
Known for: Originally rejected Jesus because He was from Nazareth. Later said Jesus was indeed the Son of God!

Name: James
Son of: Alphaeus
Note: Not the author of the book of James!

Name: Judas Iscariot
Special quality: Was the treasurer of the group (money was important to him!)
Known for: Betrayed Jesus, then committed suicide.

Jesus' Miracles

Jesus did many miracles. Miracles don't just happen on their own, such as:

✳ storms abruptly stopping (Matthew 8:23-27)

✳ water turning to wine (John 2:1-11)

✳ people coming back to life after they are dead (one example: John 11:1-44)

Jesus did four kinds of miracles. He did miracles that showed He was more powerful than nature. He did miracles that showed He was more powerful than sickness. He did miracles that showed He was more powerful than evil spirits. He did miracles that showed He was more powerful than death!

Jesus' first miracle was turning water into wine at a wedding. That showed Jesus' power over nature.

☞ Do It

Here is a list of some of Jesus' miracles. Put an N by each miracle that shows that Jesus is more powerful than nature. Put an S by the ones that show Jesus is more powerful than sickness. Put an ES by the miracles that show that Jesus is more powerful than evil spirits and put a D by the ones that show Jesus' power over death.

_____ **1. Jesus walks on the water.**

_____ **2. Jesus raises Jairus' daughter from the dead.**

_____ **3. Jesus heals the child with a demon.**

_____ **4. Jesus heals a deaf man.**

_____ **5. Jesus calms the storm.**

_____ **6. Jesus heals Peter's mother-in-law.**

_____ **7. Jesus raises Lazarus from the dead.**

_____ **8. Jesus heals a man at the pool.**

_____ **9. Jesus feeds 5,000.**

_____ **10. Jesus heals a man who could not talk because of a demon.**

Answers

1. N   2. D   3. ES   4. S   5. N
6. S   7. D   8. S   9. N   10. ES

 # Read It

Jesus Feeds the 5,000 (Matthew 14:14-21)

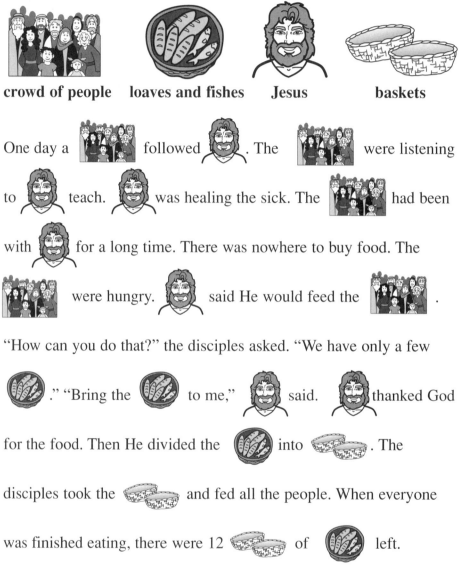

crowd of people   loaves and fishes   Jesus   baskets

One day a [crowd] followed [Jesus]. The [crowd] were listening to [Jesus] teach. [Jesus] was healing the sick. The [crowd] had been with [Jesus] for a long time. There was nowhere to buy food. The [crowd] were hungry. [Jesus] said He would feed the [crowd].

"How can you do that?" the disciples asked. "We have only a few [loaves and fishes]." "Bring the [loaves and fishes] to me," [Jesus] said. [Jesus] thanked God for the food. Then He divided the [loaves and fishes] into [baskets]. The disciples took the [baskets] and fed all the people. When everyone was finished eating, there were 12 [baskets] of [loaves and fishes] left.

A Walk on Water

After Jesus did this miracle, another miracle happened when He walked on water. You can read about it for yourself.

 Read It

Read Matthew 14:22-31 then
answer the questions below.

Where did Jesus go after the
crowd left? Why? (verse 23)

_____

_____

Where were the disciples? (verse 24)

_____

Jesus went to the disciples walking on water. How did they feel?
What did they think that Jesus was? (verse 26)

_____

What did Peter ask Jesus to let him do? (verse 28)

_____

What happened? (verse 30)

_____

What did Jesus do? (verse 31)

_____

Sometimes it is easy to become afraid or to doubt just like Peter did.
Can you think of a time you doubted God or you were afraid to do
what you knew you should do? What did you do about it?

_____

_____

The Leper's Thanks (Luke 17:11-19)

One time as Jesus was traveling, 10 men with leprosy came to Him to be healed. Leprosy is a skin disease. People did not like to be around those with leprosy, so the 10 men had to live away from their families.

The 10 men called out, "Jesus, Master, have pity on us."

Jesus said, "Go, show yourselves to the priest."

As they walked to show themselves to the priest, they were healed. One of the men who saw that he was healed ran back to Jesus and thanked Him.

Jesus asked him, "Were not all 10 cleansed? Where are the others?"

The other men didn't bother to go back and thank Jesus.

Even today we sometimes forget to be thankful for what we have and for the blessings that God gives us. Think of five things for which you are thankful and list them below.

1. _____

2. _____

3. _____

4. _____

5. _____

Make It

Leaf Print Cards

It's important to thank God. It is also important to thank those around you for what they do for you or give you. Do you remember to thank your mom or dad for cooking your meals? Do you thank your Sunday school teacher for teaching you each Sunday? Do you thank your schoolteacher for explaining a hard math problem to you? Do you thank your brother or sister for helping you with your jobs around the house? Here are some cards to make and use as thank-you notes for the people in your life.

What You Need

* leaves
* plain note cards
* washable poster paint
* paintbrush
* scrap paper
* newspaper

What to Do

1. Spread out the newspaper on your work area.
2. Lay a leaf flat on the newspaper and spread paint on it.
3. Press the leaf, painted side down, on the scrap paper.
4. Practice on scrap paper until you can make a good leaf print.
5. Decorate the front of the note cards with leaf prints in your choices of colors.
6. Let the card dry, then write your thank-you notes.

Sponge Print Cards

What You Need

* sponges
* small bowls or containers
* scrap paper
* washable poster paint
* colorful pens
* newspaper

What to Do

1. Spread out the newspaper on your work area.
2. Pour a small amount of paint in a bowl.
3. Cut sponges into different shapes.

4. Dip the sponge in the paint and then press it on the scrap paper.

5. Practice until you can make a good print.

6. Decorate the front of the note cards with sponge prints.

7. Allow to dry, then write your thank-you note.

Be like the one thankful man who was healed, not like the nine who didn't say thanks!

More Miracles

There are many more miracles you can read about in your Bible. Here are some suggestions:

Jesus feeds the 4,000   Matthew 15:32-39 or Mark 8:1-9

Jesus gets money from a fish   Matthew 17:24-27

Jesus heals the man lowered   Matthew 9:1-8 or Mark 2:1-12
through the roof   or Luke 5:17-26. (Read it from all
                                      three and compare how each writer
                                      tells the story differently.)

The Sermon on the Mount

While Jesus traveled and did miracles, He also taught about God. Sometimes He preached. Other times, He told stories.

The Sermon on the Mount is one of Jesus' most well-known sermons. It begins with nine sentences that all start with "Blessed are." These are called the Beatitudes. You might think of them as the "be-attitudes" because they are ways we should try to be!

Find Matthew 5:3-11 in your Bible. Finish each sentence on the next page. (If you are not using an NIV Bible, some of the words may be different than shown.)

Blessed are the poor in spirit, _____

_____

Blessed are those who mourn, _____

_____

Blessed are the meek, _____

_____

Blessed are those who hunger and thirst for righteousness, _____

_____

Blessed are the merciful, _____

_____

Blessed are the pure in heart, _____

_____

Blessed are the peacemakers, _____

_____

Blessed are those who are persecuted because of righteousness,

_____

Blessed are you when people _____

_____

What do those verses mean? They mean that these are the people who will be blessed or happy. Those who:

* Are spiritually needy
* Are sad
* Are free from pride
* Are seeking what is right
* Show mercy
* Have pure hearts
* Make peace
* Suffer for doing what is right
* Are made fun of for doing what is right

Does that mean you will only be blessed if you are going through bad times? No! Just the opposite, in fact. Jesus wants us to know that even in our bad times–when we are sad or suffering–He is there to bless us. It is often when we are going through a bad time that we become closer to Jesus because we spend more time in prayer.

In this same Sermon on the Mount, Jesus taught about prayer. He gave a wonderful prayer. Most churches call it "The Lord's Prayer."

"Our father in heaven, hallowed be your name, your kingdom come, your will be done on earth as it is in heaven. Give us today our daily bread. Forgive us our debts, as we also have forgiven our debtors, And lead us not into temptation, but deliver us from the evil one." ~Matthew 6:9-13

 **Do It**

Do you know what all the words mean in The Lord's Prayer? Match the part on the left with its meaning on the right. Answers are on page 147.

Our Father in heaven	Take care of our needs each day
Hallowed be your name	Forgive our sins and help us to forgive other people for what they do to us
Your kingdom come	Help Satan to not have power over us
Your will be done on earth as it is in heaven	May Your name always be holy
Give us today our daily bread	What You want done should be done both in heaven and on earth
Forgive us our debts as we also have forgiven our debtors	Keep us from doing wrong things
And lead us not into temptation	God is our loving heavenly father
But deliver us from the evil one	The Holy Spirit comes to cleanse us

Jesus' Parables

When Jesus preached, sometimes people didn't listen closely to what He said. Other times they did listen but they didn't understand. Jesus wanted to make sure they understood the important messages He was sharing, so He often told stories to make it easier for people to understand the lessons. Your pastor probably tells stories as part of the sermon at your church, too.

Jesus based His stories on ideas related to average people, such as planting crops. In one parable, He told of a farmer who took a handful of seeds and tossed them on the ground. Some seed fell on good ground and grew. Some fell on rocky ground that didn't have enough soil and the seeds couldn't grow. Some seed fell among thorns and was choked. Jesus used this to teach people about God's word. Those who listen and obey are like the seed that fell on good ground and grew.

Jesus' parables were stories that took place here on earth, but they always had deeper meanings about God.

Jesus told other stories about fishing, money, feasts and people. Here are some other parables for you to look up and read.

※ The Valuable Pearl   Matthew 13:45-46

※ The Fishing Net   Matthew 13:47-50

※ The Good Samaritan   Luke 10:30-37

※ The Prodigal Son   Luke 15:11-32

Jesus' Last Week

Jesus taught and healed people for about three years. Some people believed in Him, but others hated Him. They didn't want to hear that they were sinners. They didn't believe that Jesus was God's Son.

The gospels tell a lot about Jesus' last week on earth. Let's take a look at what happened during that special week.

Sunday   As Jesus and the disciples got near Jerusalem, Jesus told His disciples to get Him a donkey to ride. They placed their cloaks on the donkey for Jesus to sit on. The crowd along the road wanted to see Jesus. They spread their cloaks on the road. They cut branches from trees and placed them on the road also. (Matthew 21:1-11; Mark 11:1-10; Luke 19:29-44; John 12:12-19)

☞ Do It

What did the crowd of people say as Jesus passed by? Write the letter in the alphabet that comes between the two letters given to find out.

_____   _____   _____   _____

GI NP RT ZB MO MO ZB   SU NP   SU GI DF   RT NP MO

_____   _____   _____   _____

NP EG   CE ZB UW HJ CE!   AC KM DF RT RT DF CE   HJ RT

_____   _____   _____   _____   _____

GI DF   VX GI NP   BD NP LN DF RT   HJ MO   SU GI DF

_____   _____   _____   _____

MO ZB LN DF   NP EG   SU GI DF   KM NP QS CE!

_____   _____   _____   _____

GI NP RT ZB MO MO ZB   HJ MO   SU GI DF   GI HJ FH GI DF RT SU!

The solution is on the next page.

Answer: "Hosanna to the Son of David!"
"Blessed is he who comes in the name of
the Lord!" "Hosanna in the highest!"
Matthew 21:9

Monday

Jesus went to the temple and found people buying and selling things there. He tipped over the tables and drove out the salespeople  because they were doing business in God's house. (Matthew 21:12-13)

Tuesday

Jesus taught in the temple. (Matthew 21:28–23:39)

Wednesday

Judas went to the chief priest and asked what the chief priest would give him to betray Jesus. They agreed on  30 silver coins. (Matthew 26:14-16)

Thursday

Jesus shared a last supper with His disciples. Jesus told them that one of them would betray Him, but none of them (except Judas!) believed that would happen. Later that night, Jesus went to Gethsemane to pray. He was full of sorrow because He knew it was almost time to die for our sins. (Matthew 26:17-46)

Friday Early Friday morning, Jesus was arrested and put on trial at the Sanhedrin court. Later, He was judged to die by Pilate. That same day, Jesus was nailed to a cross, and He died. He was buried and a large stone was rolled in front of His tomb. Guards were placed in front of it. (Matthew 26:47–27:26)

Saturday Jesus was in the tomb.

Sunday Early in the morning, Mary and Mary Magdalene went to the tomb. There was an earthquake and the stone was rolled back. An angel told the two Marys not to be afraid. The angel told them that Jesus was alive again! How happy the women must have been! They hurried away. As they went, they saw Jesus. They fell at His feet and worshipped Him. Two more people saw Jesus on the road, and then He appeared to His disciples. Everyone was happy that Jesus was alive again. But Jesus' enemies said He wasn't really alive. They said that Jesus' followers stole His body to make it look like He rose again. But Jesus' followers knew the truth! (Matthew 28:1-10)

Chapter Eight

Apostles in Action

Acts

Luke wrote Acts. He was involved in some of the activities about which he wrote.

Acts is an exciting book about the early church. It tells about people who believed Jesus was the savior and about those who tried to harm the early believers. Stephen, Peter, Paul and several other brave and adventurous early Christians are the main characters in Acts.

Forty days after Jesus rose from the dead, He went back to heaven. The disciples were told to wait for the Holy Spirit to give them power. On a day we call "Pentecost," they received the special blessing from the Holy Spirit and were then ready to begin the church. (Acts 2:1-47)

Jesus' followers (they weren't called Christians yet) met together to sing, pray and listen to sermons. Peter became a bold preacher. The disciples also were able to heal people with God's help.

One day, Peter and John walked into the court of the temple. A crippled beggar asked them for money. Peter told him that he didn't have money, but that he could heal him in Jesus' name. The man jumped to his feet and began praising God. He attracted such a crowd that Peter and John stopped to preach to the people about Jesus.

The Sadducees (the wealthy men who controlled the priesthood) didn't believe that Jesus rose from the dead. The Sadducees got mad when Jesus' followers preached. They threw Peter and John into prison (Acts 4:18-23). The people all saw that the man was healed, but the Sadducees didn't  want to believe that Peter did it in Jesus' name. Peter and John were ordered to stop preaching, but they didn't.

More and more people believed in Jesus and soon there were 5,000 believers. People came from all over to be healed by Peter. The Jewish leaders who didn't believe in Jesus became so upset that they put Peter and John in prison again. This time, an angel of the Lord let them out and they were soon back to preaching. (Acts 5:17-26)

One of Jesus' followers was named Stephen. He preached and did miracles. The leaders didn't like Stephen, so they found people to lie about him. You can read about him for yourself.

 Read It

Read Acts 6:8-15 and 7:54-60, then answer the questions.

What did Stephen do? (verse 8)

_____

What were people told to say (lie) about Stephen? (verse 11)

_____

What did Stephen's face look like to the Sanhedrin? (verse 15)

_____

Stephen preached a long sermon to the Sanhedrin and others. He told them that their beliefs and their actions were wrong. They didn't like to hear that.

How did the Sanhedrin feel after Stephen spoke to them? (verse 54)

_____

What did Stephen see? (verse 56)

_____

What did they do to Stephen? (verse 58)

_____

What did Stephen say to the Lord? (verse 59-60)

Stephen was the first believer to be martyred (killed for his beliefs) in the New Testament. Sometimes it is hard to stand up for our beliefs. When it's hard, we can think about Stephen and other great Christians in the book of Acts who stood strong for Jesus.

When is it hard for you to stand up for your beliefs?

As Stephen was being stoned, a man named Saul was there (Acts 7:57-60). Saul's job was to hold the robes of those throwing the stones so they could throw better. Saul thought he was doing the right thing. Later, he found out he was very wrong!

Things got worse for the Christians. They were put in jail and treated poorly. Because of this, many of them moved away from Jerusalem to other cities. In a way, that was good because they started telling people in those cities about Jesus. There were now believers in many cities.

Saul heard that there were many believers in Damascus, about 200 miles from Jerusalem. The Sanhedrin had power over the Jews anywhere in the Empire. They instructed Saul to go to Damascus and arrest Jesus' followers. He planned to bring them back to Jerusalem and put them in jail.

God had a different plan for Saul. As Saul walked down the road to Damascus, a bright light shone from heaven (Acts 9:1-19). Saul fell to the ground. Then he heard a voice say, "Saul, Saul, why do you persecute me?" It was Jesus talking to Saul! He told Saul to go into the city.

👉 Do It

When Saul got up from the ground, what had happened to him? Use the clocks below to help you find the answer.

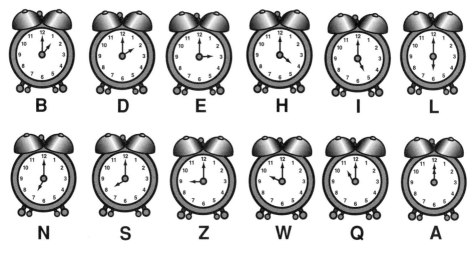

B   D   E   H   I   L

N   S   Z   W   Q   A

_____   _____   _____
4:00 3:00   10:00 12:00 8:00   1:00 6:00 5:00 7:00 2:00 .

Answer: He was blind (Acts 9:8-9).

God told a man named Ananias to go to Saul and talk to him. Ananias wasn't sure he wanted to do that. He had heard about Saul and was afraid of what he might to do to him! God told Ananias that Saul would become a follower of Jesus and would suffer for Jesus. Ananias went to Saul and healed him, and Saul was filled with the Holy Spirit in Jesus' name.

God changed Saul's name to Paul. Now, instead of harming the believers, Paul was one of them. He began preaching about Jesus!

Until this time, the Gospel was only preached to the Jews. God used a vision to tell Peter that it was time to take Jesus' story to the Gentiles, people who were not Jews. A Gentile named Cornelius wanted to hear about Jesus so Peter went to his house. At first, the Jews weren't sure that this was a good idea because Jews didn't associate with Gentiles. But Peter told them that Cornelius became a believer and that the Holy Spirit came to him. Now the gospel would be spread to all people, Jews and Gentiles!

Make It

Cross Necklace

Peter, Paul and other followers of Jesus preached to crowds of people. They told them that Jesus died on the cross and rose again. You can make a cross necklace to wear to remind you that Jesus died on the cross for you. The nails will remind you of the nails that pierced Jesus' hand. The ribbon will remind you of the blood that Jesus shed. If someone asks you about your necklace, share the good news about Jesus just as the early Christians did.

What You Need

* two short nails   ✳ two long nails
* copper wire   ✳ wire cutters or scissors
* red ribbon

What to Do

1. You can buy two nails of each size at a hardware store. Try using 1½-inch nails for the short ones and 2½-inch for the long ones. You will need four pieces of copper wire that are about 7" and one piece that is about 11".

2. Place the two short nails side by side facing opposite ways. A sharp point and a head will be side by side. Wrap a short piece of wire around each end to hold them together. You might want to have a parent help you to tightly wrap the wire.

3. Place the two long nails side by side facing opposite ways. Wrap a short piece of wire around each end to hold them together.

4. Place the short nails across the long nails to form a cross. Crisscross the long piece of wire to hold them together to fit around your neck.

5. Measure and cut a length of ribbon that fits around your neck. Place the cross in the middle of the ribbon. Secure it by knotting the ribbon around it or loop the ribbon through the top wiring on the cross.

6. Tie the ends of the ribbon together to form a necklace.

For a few years, the gospel message was spread without much persecution. Then King Herod Agrippa started harming the believers. He killed James, John's brother. He put Peter in prison, but an angel let him out.

At the same time that this was happening in Jerusalem, Paul was in Antioch, about 350 miles north of Jerusalem. It was here that the believers were called Christians for the first time. From here, Paul and another Christian named Barnabas started on a long trip to take the gospel to other places. This was called a "missionary journey" and it was the first of three missionary journeys that Paul made.

Here is what happened to Paul and Barnabas on their trip (Acts 13:1–14:28):

✳ They taught in the Jewish synagogues.

✳ Paul made Elymas, a wicked sorcerer, become blind when he tried to keep others from believing in Jesus.

✳ Paul healed a lame man and the people thought Paul and Barnabas were gods and bowed to them.

✳ They fled to keep from getting stoned to death.

✳ Paul eventually did get stoned and dragged out of the city because the people thought he was dead.

Then Paul and Barnabas went back to Antioch and taught there for a while before planning another trip. But Paul and Barnabas had a disagreement. Barnabas wanted to take John Mark with them on their second journey. Paul didn't want to take him because John Mark had been with them earlier and then left them. They had such an argument that Paul took Silas, another believer, with him on his second journey instead of Barnabas.

Here is what happened on Paul's second missionary journey (Acts 15:40–18:28):

✳ Paul and Silas met a young believer named Timothy. Two books of the Bible are written to him.

✳ Paul had a vision of a man in Macedonia calling to him.

✳ Lydia, a seller of purple cloth, became a believer and was baptized.

✳ Paul made an evil spirit leave a girl. Some men owned the girl and used her as a fortuneteller. Now she could not do her job and they were angry.

✳ Paul and Silas were thrown into prison. They sang and praised God. The jailer became a believer.

✳ An angry mob started a riot in Thessalonica.

✳ In Athens, Paul talked to people who worshipped idols.

✳ Paul met Aquila and Priscilla, who were tent makers like he was. He stayed with them in Corinth.

Sometimes Paul felt discouraged, but he knew God would take care of him. What are some times when you feel discouraged?

Paul stayed in Corinth for a while. Then he decided to start his third missionary journey. Here is what happened on it (Acts 19:1-20:38):

❋ The believers in Ephesus received the Holy Spirit.

❋ Demetrius, an idolmaker, started a riot because he didn't want the people to believe in Jesus or no one would buy his idols.

❋ A young man named Eutychus was listening to Paul while sitting in a third story window when he fell out the window and died! Paul raised him from the dead.

 Answer It

The early Christians told others about their faith. Not everyone did this in the same way. Today we each share our faith in the way that is most comfortable to us. Read the sentences in each fish. Check all of the sentences that describe you and your personality. They will help you know the best way to share your faith.

Fish 1

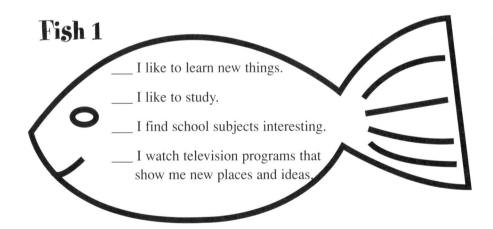

_____ I like to learn new things.

_____ I like to study.

_____ I find school subjects interesting.

_____ I watch television programs that show me new places and ideas.

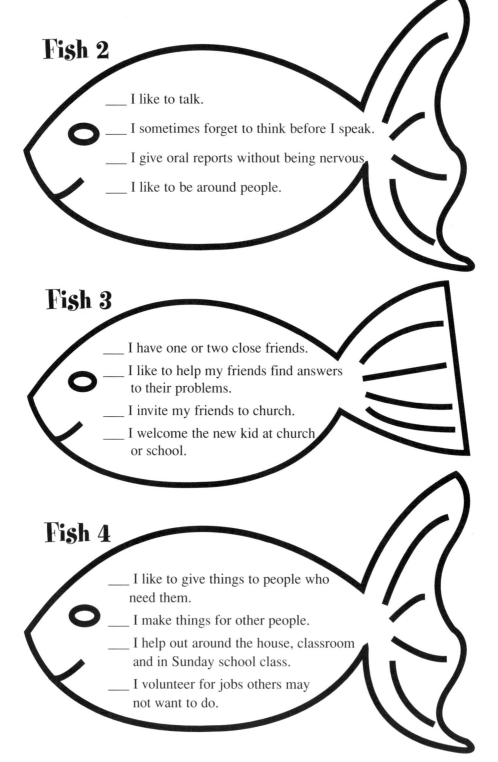

Fish 2

___ I like to talk.

___ I sometimes forget to think before I speak.

___ I give oral reports without being nervous.

___ I like to be around people.

Fish 3

___ I have one or two close friends.

___ I like to help my friends find answers to their problems.

___ I invite my friends to church.

___ I welcome the new kid at church or school.

Fish 4

___ I like to give things to people who need them.

___ I make things for other people.

___ I help out around the house, classroom and in Sunday school class.

___ I volunteer for jobs others may not want to do.

In which fish did you check the most sentences?

Fish 1: You are like the Apostle Paul, who liked to think about things. When he talked to others about Jesus, Paul tried to use logic and make them understand. When you talk to others about Jesus, you do the same by explaining the meanings of different Bible verses. You enjoy reading books about the Bible, Bible times and places.

Fish 2: You are like Peter, who preached to large crowds (Acts 2). Sometimes Peter acted without thinking, such as when he denied Jesus three times (John 19:15-27). But Peter was also brave and spoke freely to thousands about Jesus. You are brave in suggesting activities such as praying around the school flag pole, or in sharing your faith by giving an oral book report on a missionary biography.

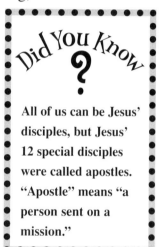

Did You Know?

All of us can be Jesus' disciples, but Jesus' 12 special disciples were called apostles. "Apostle" means "a person sent on a mission."

Fish 3: You are like Andrew, who brought people one by one to Jesus. He brought his brother Peter (John 1:40-42). He brought the little boy with the loaves and fish (John 6:8-9). Andrew was different from Peter. Andrew didn't speak to large crowds. He wasn't impulsive or loud. He saw people who had needs and tried to solve the needs one by one. You share your faith by asking one friend at a time to church or telling one friend at a time about Jesus.

Fish 4: You are like Dorcas, who shared her faith by her good works. She helped the poor (Acts 9:36). You show God's love by helping others with homework and jobs. Try baking cookies for a busy mom or a nursing home visit!

Paul returned to Jerusalem (Acts 21:17–26:32). Some people thought he was teaching against the laws. They took him to jail. Soldiers took him to Caesarea to keep him from being killed by the angry mob. Paul talked to Felix, the governor, about his beliefs. Paul was still kept as a prisoner.

Festus took over for Felix. Paul told Festus about his beliefs. He also got to tell King Agrippa about how he met Jesus. Paul demanded that he be allowed to see Caesar, the Roman Emperor. On the way to Rome, Paul's ship was wrecked but everyone made it safely to an island. A snake there bit Paul, but God kept him safe. Paul was taken to Rome and kept a prisoner in a house for two years. Even during this time he preached and told others about Jesus (Acts 27:1–28:30).

The Bible doesn't tell us what happened to Paul but history says that he was declared "not guilty" and allowed to go free. He continued his missionary work by going to Spain. Later he was arrested again and this time he was killed for his beliefs.

In the next section, you will read many letters that Paul wrote. They later became books of the Bible.

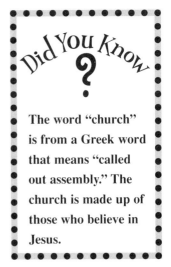

Did You Know?

The word "church" is from a Greek word that means "called out assembly." The church is made up of those who believe in Jesus.

Chapter Nine

Learning from the Letters

The epistles are letters written to certain Bible times people or churches. Sometimes the letter told the people or churches what they were doing wrong or it told them how to act. Other times a letter encouraged them. Epistles also were written to teach the people more about the Christian life or how to run a church.

Even though these letters were written to the early Christians, the lessons and advice in them still relate to us today.

Romans

Paul wrote this letter to the Christians in Rome five or six years before he was taken there as a prisoner. Rome–now a large city in Italy–was a busy and exciting place even then. It was built on seven flat hills east of the Tiber River. There were about 1 million people living there, half of them slaves. The people in Rome were either rich or very poor.

When Paul wrote this letter, Nero was emperor of Rome. He was a wicked man. He even killed his own mother!

Christians in Rome were persecuted. That means they were treated very badly for being Christians. The Christians hid in long tunnels and rooms– called catacombs–they had dug in the soft rock under the city. There were about 600 miles of catacombs under Rome!

The book of Romans told the people how to become Christians. Paul explained that Jesus died for the sins of everyone in the world, and that faith is what saves us.

1 & 2 Corinthians

Paul wrote these letters to the church in Corinth, an important city in Greece. Travelers and merchants passed through Corinth to get to other places. The people there worshipped idols and built temples for their idols. They did many sinful things.

The Christians in Corinth had problems. They argued a lot and were often angry with each other. Paul wrote to teach them how to live as Jesus' followers. He told them that the church is made up of a lot of different people, just as their human bodies were made up of many different parts. Paul explained that they needed to love each other.

In 1 Corinthians 13, which is known as the "love chapter" of the Bible, Paul taught that love is patient and that it looks for the good in other people. Love doesn't brag and doesn't always have to have its own way. Love is polite and doesn't get angry or keep track of other people's mistakes.

In his second letter to the Corinthians, Paul told the Christians to help others in need. He warned them about false teachers who would try to turn them away from Jesus.

Memorize It

Love is patient, love is kind. It does not envy, it does not boast, it is not proud. It is not rude, it is not self-seeking, it is not easily angered, it keeps no record of wrongs. Love does not delight in evil but rejoices with the truth. It always protects, always trusts, always hopes, always perseveres.

~1 Corinthians 13:4-7

Make It

Heart Necklace

Here is a craft to remind you to love others. Make it and then give it to someone who is special to you. You can also make magnets or pins instead of necklaces.

What You Need

✳ Crayola Model Magic®
✳ heart-shaped cookie cutter
✳ yarn, safety pin or magnet
✳ paint
✳ paintbrush
✳ pencil
✳ sealable plastic sandwich bag

What to Do

1. Roll the Crayola Model Magic® to between ⅛" and ¼" thick.
2. Use the cookie cutter to cut the desired shaped. Put the unused Crayola Model Magic® in a sealable plastic bag to keep it fresh.
3. Push a pencil through the top portion of the shape to make a hole in which to string the yarn.
4. Allow to dry for several hours.
5. Paint and decorate.
6. String yarn through the hole for a necklace, glue a safety pin on the back for a pin or glue a magnet on the back for a refrigerator magnet.

Galatians

Paul wrote this book to the churches in Galatia, an area that is now part of the country of Turkey. He had visited Galatia during his second missionary journey and had started many churches there.

Paul told the people that only believing in Jesus could save them from their sins. Paul also explained it was not necessary to become a Jew before becoming a Christian.

What a person is like inside is important, isn't it? In Galatians, Paul gave us a special list of what we should have on the inside. (These are good characteristics to look for in friends also!) You can find the list–called "the Fruit of the Spirit"–in Galatians 5:22-23. They are called the Fruit of the Spirit because when we let God's spirit guide us, they will be a part of us.

✝ Memorize It

But the fruit of the spirit is love, joy, peace, patience, kindness, goodness, faithfulness, gentleness, and self-control. Against such things there is no law.

~Galatians 5:22-23

☞ Do It

Do you know what each of those words means? Try to match the word on this page to its definition on the next page. Put the correct letter in front of each word.

___ **1. love**   ___ **2. joy**

___ **3. peace**   ___ **4. patience**

___ **5. kindness**   ___ **6. goodness**

___ **7. faithfulness** ___ **8. gentleness**

___ **9. self-control**

a. **putting up with annoyance without complaining**

b. **having positive and desirable qualities**

c. **control over emotions and behavior**

d. **strong affection for another**

e. **helpful and considerate**

f. **loyal**

g. **feeling of great happiness**

h. **calm feeling**

i. **kind and thoughtful, tender**

Answers

1. d   2. g   3. h   4. a   5. e

6. b   7. f   8. i   9. c

If you got some of them mixed up, that's okay. Some of the definitions are similar. The purpose of the quiz is to get you thinking about the top nine character traits that are important to God. Are these what you see in yourself? Are they what you look for when choosing a friend?

Read the following stories. Decide which character trait the friend is displaying in the story and write it on the line.

Shayna and Nicole, both 11, had been friends since first grade. After lunch, Tara, another fifth-grader, asked Shayna to sit next to her.

"Why don't you come to my house tonight? I know you always go to Nicole's house but my house is bigger," Tara bragged. "And besides, we can use my computer to do our homework. When we're done I have lots of Nintendo games to play. I bet Nicole doesn't have a computer of her own and Nintendo games."

"I like doing my homework with Nicole," said Shayna. "She's

nice, and she doesn't mind helping me when I get stuck on my math homework. You can come and study with us at Nicole's house. We can all work together."

"No, thanks," sneered Tara. "You can either be my friend or Nicole's friend. I don't plan to be friends with Nicole. Her family is poor."

"I am not going to stop being friends with Nicole just because you have more stuff than she does. That's not what is important to me," Shayna said.

Which Fruit of the Spirit is Shayna displaying?

Abby and Michaela were working on their math homework.

"When we get done we can watch the new video my mom bought," Abby said. "I can't wait to see it."

"I'm never going to get done," Michaela wailed. "I just don't understand how to add and subtract fractions. My answers  aren't coming out right at all. Look, my answer is 4/5 and that's not even one of the three choices!"

"I see your mistake. Here, let me show you again," Abby said. "Now you try the next one."

Michaela worked for a few minutes and then slammed down her pencil. "I just don't get it," she said. "Why don't you go ahead and watch the video. I'm never going to get done!"

"You can do it," Abby said. "Here, let me show you again."

Which Fruit of the Spirit is Abby displaying?

Carrie walked to a lunchroom table with her tray. She sat it down, then took her place with the other girls.

"Look," snickered Lori. "There's that new girl, Brittany. She must get her clothes at a thrift store."

"I think she's nice," said Carrie. "She's just a little shy."

Just then Brittany bumped into a boy and dropped her tray.

"What a klutz," Lori said.

Carrie ignored Lori and went to help Brittany.

"Anyone could drop a tray," Carrie told Lori. "Let's get you a new one and then you and I can sit together."

What Fruit of the Spirit did Carrie display?

If you said that Shayna was faithful, or we might call it loyal, then you were right. If you make friends with people because of who they are on the inside, then you won't dump them for someone who has more toys, games, clothes or other things.

If you guessed that Abby was patient, then you were right. If someone is your friend, you won't mind taking the extra time to help her with a hard task or to wait for her to do something. And she should do the same for you!

Did you say that Carrie was kind? You're right. Carrie showed kindness to someone with whom she wasn't friends yet. She stood up to Lori and helped Brittany.

Now it's your turn. Write an ending to this story that shows love.

"I can't wait until the party at Jenny's house Saturday," Daphni said to Kaylee. "It's going to be great."

"I can't go," Kaylee said. "My grandma's sick and we might have to go visit her at her house."

"And miss the party?" Daphni asked.

"Yes. My dad says, 'There'll be other parties but there's only one Gran.' He won't let me stay home but he said you could come with us and we could order a pizza. You would probably rather go to the party though," Kaylee said.

_____

_____

_____

These are only four of the nine Fruit of the Spirit. The other five are just as important. Think about these character traits as you talk with your friends this week.

Ephesians

Paul wrote a letter to the church at Ephesus while he was in prison in Rome. Ephesus was the most important city in the area that is now Turkey. Many traders passed through it. Ephesus had a big temple for worshipping the Roman goddess Diana.

Paul used a lot of the letter to tell the people of the wonderful blessings they have in Christ. Then he told the Ephesians how they should live as Christians.

In the last chapter of his letter, Paul talked about how parents and children should get along. Children are told to honor and obey their parents. Fathers are told to raise their children to live for the Lord. Do you and your parents always get along? There are probably times when you don't  like what they tell you to do and their decisions. There probably are times when your parents get upset with you as well.

Make It

Family Fun

Talk to your parents about having a special family night to talk about any problems you might be having. Then make one or more of the snacks below to share while you spend time together. Pour the ingredients listed into a bag or bowl for sharing and just mix or shake.

Sweet Family Mix

1 cup plain M&Ms®

1 cup peanut M&Ms®

1 cup white chocolate chips

1 cup gummy bears

1 cup malted milk balls

Pretzel Mix

1 cup plain M&Ms®

1 cup miniature marshmallows

1 cup pretzel sticks

½ cup peanuts or sunflower seeds

Healthy Mix

1 cup cubed hard cheese

1 cup peanuts

1 cup cubed turkey

½ cup sunflower seeds

Kabobs are fun, and easy to make! Just thread the ingredients on the next page on a wood or metal kabob stick.

Fruit Kabobs

Kiwi squares

Strawberry halves

Pineapple chunks

Sandwich Kabobs

Lunch meat cubes

Cheese cubes

Bread squares

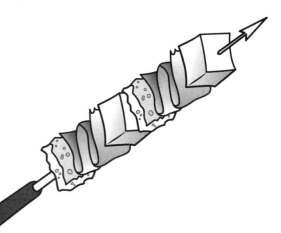

After trying some of these ideas, create your own mixes and kabobs. See who can come up with the most creative ones!

✝ Memorize It

Children, obey your parents in the Lord, for this is right. "Honor your father and mother" – which is the first commandment with a promise – "that it may go well with you and that you may enjoy long life on the earth."

~Ephesians 6:1-3

Philippians

Paul may have written this letter to the church in Philippi during the two years that he was a prisoner in his house in Rome. During that time, Philippi was a rich Roman colony. There were probably not many Jews living there.

The book of Philippians is a book of joy. Paul told the church to always be happy and to rejoice. He said they would find joy by telling others about Jesus, by caring for each other, by pleasing Jesus and by trusting Jesus in everything.

✝ Memorize It

Rejoice in the Lord always. I will say it again: Rejoice!

~Philippians 4:4

Colossians

Like with Philippians, Paul may have written this book to the church in Colosse while a prisoner in his house. The Colossian church was a Gentile (non-Jewish) church. In earlier times, Colosse had been an important city in what is now Turkey, but by the time Paul  wrote his letter it had lost its importance. Epaphras, a man who had become a Christian when Paul taught in Ephesus, took the letter to Colosse for Paul.

False teachers were telling the people in the Colossian church that they had to worship angels, take part in Jewish ceremonies and do some other wrong things. Paul wrote the letter to tell them that they had to worship and serve Jesus only. Jesus is the only way to salvation.

✝ Memorize It

And whatever you do, whether in word or deed, do it all in the name of the Lord Jesus, giving thanks to God the Father through him.
~Colossians 3:17

1 & 2 Thessalonians

Paul wrote these letters to the church in Thessalonica, a busy seaport. When Paul started the church there, he was thrown out of the city so quickly that he had little time to teach the Thessalonians about Christianity.

Paul's friend Timothy had told Paul that the people were sad because some Christians had died. In 1 Thessalonians, Paul told them that one day they will see their Christian friends who had died. He also told them that Jesus will come again one day.

When they read Paul's letter, the Thessalonians misunderstood and decided that if Jesus was coming again they might as well not bother going to work or doing what they needed to do. When Paul heard about this, he wrote a second letter (2 Thessalonians) telling them that they needed to keep working and living well because we do not know when Jesus will return.

✝ Memorize It

Make sure that nobody pays back wrong for wrong, but always try to be kind to each other and to everyone else.
~1 Thessalonians 5:15

1 & 2 Timothy

Paul wrote these letters to Timothy, a young man who was in charge of the church at Ephesus and who had been with Paul during some of his work. Timothy was from Lystra. His father was a Gentile. His mother was a Jew who believed in Jesus. Timothy had been taught the scriptures all of his life. Paul wanted to visit Timothy, but he couldn't. So he wrote him letters to help him be a good leader for the Ephesian church.

In his first letter to Timothy, Paul warned him about false leaders. He told him how to choose good church leaders and gave him advice on how to treat people in the church. Paul encouraged Timothy to be a good example for other believers.

When Paul wrote the second letter to Timothy, Paul was in a cold dungeon. He felt lonely. Many of his friends had left him. Only Luke remained. Paul asked Timothy to come and see him and to bring Mark and the coat and scrolls he had left behind.

The second letter to Timothy encouraged him to follow the truth. Paul warned Timothy that there will be trouble and that people will turn away from God. Paul told Timothy to be a good servant of God.

✝ Memorize It

Don't let anyone look down on you because you are young, but set an example for the believers in speech, in life, in love, in faith and in purity.

~1 Timothy 4:12

 Answer It

Paul told Timothy to be a role model in his speech, in the way he lived, in love, in his faith and in purity. Are you a good role model for others in those same areas? Read the list below and put a check by each one you do.

With Your Words

_____ I use good language.

_____ I use my words to encourage others.

_____ I don't use "cut downs."

_____ I use my words to pray and praise God.

_____ I use my words to tell others about Jesus.

_____ I use my words to invite others to church.

With the Way You Live

_____ I always keep a good attitude.

_____ I am friendly to others.

_____ I am helpful to my teachers.

_____ I am helpful at home.

_____ I do my work cheerfully.

_____ I keep my temper even when losing a game.

With Your Love

_____ I show my love for my family through my actions.

_____ I show my love for God by obeying His word.

_____ I have God's love for those who aren't always kind to me.

_____ I show my love to my friends by being unselfish.

_____ I show my love for siblings by being patient.

_____ I ask God to help me love others.

With Your Faith

_____ I listen in my church class.

_____ I try to learn more about God by reading my Bible.

_____ I take time to pray at least a few minutes every day.

_____ I tell others about God.

_____ I encourage others to come to church.

_____ I encourage others to learn more about God.

With Your Purity

_____ I do what is right even when no one is looking.

_____ I make choices that will help me be a better person.

_____ I don't read or watch things that use bad language or talk about God in a bad way.

_____ I walk away when others are doing wrong.

_____ I try to honor God by what I do and say.

_____ I am careful of what I see, hear and do.

Did you put a check by all 30 sentences? Probably not! No one does the right thing all the time. Pick one statement from each area to work on this week.

Titus

Paul wrote this letter to Titus, a Greek who believed in Jesus. He had been with Paul on some of Paul's travels. Titus worked with the churches at Corinth and Crete. The people in Crete behaved poorly. Paul wrote this letter to Titus to help him with the church in Crete.

Paul told Titus to choose church leaders who will be examples and who will teach the right things. He told Titus to teach both the older and younger Christians to do what is right. The letter also said that fighting should end when people find out about God's love.

✝ Memorize It

But when the kindness and love of God our Savior appeared, he saved us, not because of righteous things we had done, but because of his mercy. He saved us through the washing of rebirth and renewal by the Holy Spirit.

~Titus 3:4-5

Philemon

Paul was in prison when he wrote this letter to his friend Philemon of Colosse. Paul wrote the letter to Philemon to talk about Philemon's slave, Onesimus. Onesimus had run away from Philemon. Then Onesimus met Paul and became a Christian. Paul wrote to Philemon to ask him to forgive Onesimus for running away. Paul offered to pay anything Onesimus owed Philemon. He told Philemon that he and Onesimus were brothers now because they were both Christians.

✝ Memorize It

I pray that you may be active in sharing your faith, so that you will have a full understanding of every good thing we have in Christ.
~Philemon 1:6

Hebrews

The writer of Hebrews is not known. Different people have different ideas about who wrote Hebrews. Some believe it was Paul, others think it was Barnabas, Apollos or a friend of Timothy's. Even though we don't know who wrote it, Hebrews still holds a lot of instruction for us. Hebrews was written to Jews who believed in Jesus.

The book of Hebrews shows that Jesus is greater than the prophets who spoke for God in the Old Testament. He is greater than the angels. The angels worship Jesus! He is greater than Moses, a faithful servant of God's. Jesus is greater than Joshua, who was a mighty leader. He is greater than the high priests before Him. He became the perfect sacrifice for sin.

Hebrews chapter 11 is called the "faith chapter" in the New Testament. It gives us a faith "hall of fame." Read Hebrews 11 and tell what the verses say about each of these people.

Abel

_____

Enoch

_____

Noah

_____

Abraham

_____

Isaac

_____

Jacob

_____

Joseph

_____

Moses' parents

_____

Moses

_____

Rahab

_____

What would you want God to say about you and your faith?

_____

_____

✝ Memorize It

Now faith is being sure of what we hope for and certain of what we do not see.

~Hebrews 11:1

James

James, Jesus' half-brother, wrote James. At first, James didn't believe that Jesus was the Messiah. After all, they probably grew up together just like you and your brothers and sisters. You might have trouble believing that there was something really special about one of your siblings, too!

The book of James encouraged Christians to put their faith into action. James told people that it isn't enough to read or hear the Bible–you have to live it, too. He said a faith that is only in your heart and doesn't change your actions isn't very strong.

Make It

Faith in Action

Need to put your faith in action? Do this service project with your family, friends or Sunday school class. Ask a parent to help you locate a food bank in your area that accepts donations of canned goods. Be sure to ask when the food bank accepts donations because some only take donations on particular days or during certain hours.

Invitations

Have one paper grocery sack for each friend you plan to invite. Use the sack as the invitation. On each sack write:

You're Invited!

Place

Time

Date

Please fill this sack with dry or canned goods for the food bank and bring it with you.

Taking the Food

Make sure that each friend has her parent's permission to deliver the canned food to the food bank. Ask a parent to help you find a large cardboard box. (You can usually get them at a grocery store.) Have your friends help

decorate it using markers. Put all of the food into the box and ask a parent to drive you to the food bank to deliver it.

After Delivering

Here are some fun treats you and your friends can make together after you deliver your food to the food bank.

Banana Boat

You will need an adult to help you with the oven or grill for this.

What You Need

* bananas
* peanut butter
* mini-marshmallows
* chocolate chips
* maraschino cherries
* aluminum foil
* knife

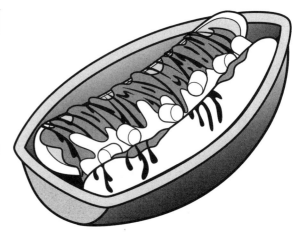

What to Do

1. Peel a banana and slice it the long way (don't cut all the way through!). After you cut it, the banana should look like a boat.

2. Coat the inside with peanut butter.

3. Sprinkle with mini-marshmallows and chocolate chips.

4. Wrap the banana in foil and ask an adult to place it in the oven at 350 degrees or on a grill just until the chocolate chips and marshmallows melt.

5. Remove and top with cherries.

6. Eat!

Sprinkle Apples

What You Need

* apples
* craft sticks
* white or dark chocolate chips
* candy sprinkles
* wax paper

What to Do

1. Clean the apple.

2. Place it on wax paper.

3. Insert a craft stick into the apple at the stem.

4. Have a parent help you microwave the chocolate on medium power until it is melted.

5. Roll the apple in the chocolate until it is coated.

6. Roll the apple in the sprinkles until coated.

7. Enjoy!

✝ Memorize It

My dear brothers, take note of this: Everyone should be quick to listen, slow to speak and slow to become angry, for man's anger does not bring about the righteous life that God desires. ~James 1:19-20

1 & 2 Peter

Peter, one of the 12 disciples, wrote these two letters. Peter had become a bold and courageous preacher for Jesus by the time he wrote these letters. (These letters were written near the end of Peter's life.) Peter wrote to Christians who were suffering for their belief in Jesus. He was suffering, too!

Peter told the early Christians that Jesus is their example. He told them to look to Jesus for help and they could have joy even when they were treated badly.

In his second letter, Peter warned Christians about false teachers. He told the Christians that Jesus would return one day. Peter said that they should try and live holy and godly lives.

✝ Memorize It

But just as he who called you is holy, so be holy in all you do; for it is written: "Be holy, because I am holy."

~1 Peter 1:15-16

1, 2 & 3 John

John, one of the 12 disciples, wrote these three short letters. These letters were probably passed from church to church in Asia

Minor. John knew Jesus well. He was one of Jesus' closest friends.

In John's first letter, he told Christians that they should live differently. He said they should "walk in the light" or try not to sin. He said they should try to live the way Jesus wants them to live. John also told the Christians that they should love one another because God loved them and sent Jesus to die for them.

John's second letter is only 13 verses long. It was written to warn the people about false teachers. John told them not to welcome any teacher who does not teach the truth about Jesus.

John wrote his third letter to Gaius, a friend who let traveling helpers stay in his home. John said he is happy that Gaius had remained faithful to Jesus. He told him to only do what is good and not be like Diotrephes, who was bossy and selfish.

✝ Memorize It

Dear friends, let us love one another, for love comes from God. Everyone who loves has been born of God and knows God.
~1 John 4:7

Jude

Jude, Jesus' relative, wrote this short letter. He wrote to warn believers about false teachers. His letter was probably passed from church to church.

Jude warned the people that those who teach lies about Jesus would be punished. He told the believers to defend the truth and to help those who are confused about the truth.

✝ Memorize It

To the only God our Savior be glory, majesty, power and authority, through Jesus Christ our Lord, before all ages, now and forevermore!
~Jude 1:25

Chapter Ten

Exciting Endtimes

Revelation

John, one of the 12 disciples, wrote this book. He also wrote the gospel of John and the three letters with his name (John 1, 2 and 3). John was on Patmos, an island in the Mediterranean Sea, when he wrote Revelation.

In Revelation, John wrote about what was to happen in the future. He said Christ will triumph and Satan will be defeated, and there will be a new heaven and earth.

The book of Revelation begins with a special message to seven churches. They were the churches at Ephesus, Smyrna, Pergamum, Thyatira, Sardis, Philadelphia and Laodicea. John wrote letters to some of the churches to praise them for being faithful. After he praised them for being faithful, he pointed out what they needed to change. In letters to the other churches he said that the people were being lazy and not working hard for Jesus. He told them to turn from their sins and live like Christians.

After the letters, John described a vision. God gave him the vision as a message to the people. In the vision, John was taken into heaven, where he saw four creatures.

☞ Do It

What did the creatures say all day and all night? Use the box code on the next page to decode the message. To find the first letter, put one finger on G and one finger on 3. Bring your fingers together. They should meet at "H" so you should write "H" for your first letter.

1	2	3	4	5	6
A	Y	B	X	C	W
T	F	U	E	V	D
G	S	H	J	I	R
P	O	N	M	L	K

————— ————— ————— ————— —————

G3 P2 P5 A2,   G3 P2 P5 A2,   G3 P2 P5 A2   G5 G2   T1 G3 T4

————— ————— ————— —————

P5 P2 G6 T6   G1 P2 T6   A1 P5 P4 G5 G1 G3 T1 A2,   A6 G3 P2

————— ————— ————— ————— ————— —————

A6 A1 G2,   A1 P3 T6   G5 G2,   A1 P3 T6   G5 G2   T1 P2

—————

A5 P2 P4 T4.

Answer: Holy, holy, holy is the Lord God Almighty, who was, and is, and is to come.
Revelation 4:8

✝ **Memorize It**

You are worthy, our Lord and God, to receive glory and honor and power, for you created all things, and by your will they were created and have their being.

~Revelation 4:11

Make It

Alpha and Omega Bracelet

Revelation 1:8 says, "'I am the Alpha and the Omega,' says the Lord God, 'who is, and who was, and who is to come, the Almighty.'"
Alpha is the first letter of the Greek alphabet. Omega is the last letter.
Jesus has always existed. He was there when God created the world.

He will be there when the new heaven and the new earth are formed for us to live in forever.

What You Need

* letter beads
* color beads (in your favorite colors with the same size hole)
* elastic that will fit through the holes

What to Do

1. Find the letters to spell out "Alpha" and "Omega."
2. Choose other beads to form a pattern.
3. Arrange them on a table until you have them the way you want them.
4. Slip elastic through all the beads.
5. Have a parent tie the elastic around your wrist tight enough that it won't slide around but loose enough to pull on and off.
6. When people ask you what "Alpha" and "Omega" mean, you can tell them about Jesus' message in the book of Revelation

As John's vision continued, he saw many things, some of which were scary, such as people with sores on their skin and rivers of blood. But even though this dream seemed more like a nightmare, Jesus gave it to John so he could tell the people there is hope. Remember, many people during John's time were suffering for their beliefs in Jesus because not many other people believed in Him yet. So Jesus wanted the people to know that even in the bad times, He would be with them.

Most importantly, Jesus wanted the people to know that in the end, God will always win over evil. Revelation closes with a reminder that Jesus will one day come again.

Puzzle Answers

Old Testament crossword, page 27

Noah's Ark crossword, page 32

Joseph crossword, page 40

Jericho crossword, page 61

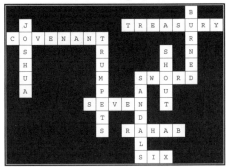

Elijah crossword, page 79

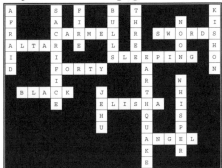

Ezra crossword, page 85

Proverbs crossword, page 97

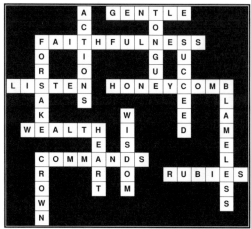

Jonah crossword, page 116

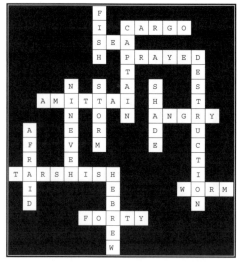

New Testament puzzle, page 126